# WHEN GLOBAL MEETS LOCAL

## How Expatriates Can Succeed in Myanmar

**A FIRST-TIME GUIDEBOOK**

**By Hana Bui**

# TABLE OF CONTENTS

# ACKNOWLEDGEMENTS

My special thanks go to Werner Eggert, the journalist and journalism trainer. He motivated me to write the book from its infancy and helped with the critical direction of the book. Moreover, he patiently read the first messy draft and then some further ones to comment on them. Both his encouragement and demand for a high-quality book have inspired me to go the extra mile. I feel indebted.

Thank you, June Saunders, the editor. Not only did she do the professional work to edit my book, but she also put her heart into working on the manuscript. I appreciate it!

Thanks to Kay, the designer who did the amazing book cover. I'm hoping that for readers it will be "love at first sight".

I acknowledge with gratitude the participation of over 100 expats in Myanmar and 50 local professionals in responding to my questionnaire for the book's survey. They are too numerous to name. I am particularly thankful to 30 professionals who were willing to have in-depth discussions with me. Their precious sharing provides the insights and authentic stories for the book. They were more than patient answering my endless interview questions.

Thank you, Ko Maung Maung Htway, the repat working in advertising sector who shared interesting thoughts on Burmese people traits.

My heartfelt thanks to my ex-librarian mother and ex-lecturer father whose careers and concerns both originated and then embraced my writing passion. Thanks to my brother for his help with the references!

My sincere thanks to my relatives and friends. At all times, their generous assistance and encouragement always warm me.

Thank you, the readers! You are the reason the book exists. Whenever I felt exhausted writing the book, I thought about my beloved readers who will benefit from it. Then I would feel inspired! I continued the journey with joy.

Finally, I shall be very thankful for any sharing from readers – comments, suggestions, and your own experience with the book.

# PREFACE

*SHIFTING SANDS AND ROCK-HARD PRINCIPLES*

Described as "the last frontier market," Myanmar opened its door in April 2011. This followed the declaration of economic reform policies by then president U Thein Sein and his quasi-civilian government.

My first visit to Myanmar was in late 2012. There were not many cars on the road. Traveling in the city of Yangon was not much of a hassle. No one said, "Sorry, I am late because of the terrible traffic," as is said so frequently today.

Anyone who knew Myanmar before it opened up would recognize the tremendous changes taking place here in recent times. Before, the internet was much more expensive, slow, and unstable. A mobile phone was a luxury – I bought my MPT sim card for 250 USD then. Before that, a sim card with a good (lucky) number would cost thousands of bucks. A local friend of mine once bought a sim card for 5,000 USD.

Following the opening of the country, the U.S. and Europe partially lifted the embargo. Then in November of 2015, the new democratic government of NLD was put in place after a landslide election victory. Since opening in 2011, Foreign

Direct Investment has poured into Myanmar, as have many international development organizations. As a result, more and more investors and expats came.

Nowadays, it costs only a dollar or so to buy a sim card. The blue, red, yellow and orange colors of Telenor, Ooredoo, MPT, and Mytel are visible on signboards at countless local shops. The internet is much faster after the communication revolution. People access their favorite social media – Facebook – and use Viber on a daily basis. Foreigners are unquestionably pleased by this because they use the Internet every minute. Leapfrogging development in economics and various areas of Myanmar will hopefully take place, thanks to the telecommunication revolution.

The streets are full of cars now, and thus traffic jams are common. There is a tsunami of new, countless enterprises, at least in Yangon. To name a few, there are new shopping centers, hotels, office buildings, condos, restaurants and bars, fast food places, beauty stores, etc.

All over the Golden Land, there is a tremendous change. However, some things have remained constant or have only changed a little. I still hear from many expats who work here how "strange" it is in working with their local colleagues. That was true for me, as well. I was a stranger in a strange land too. At the same time, local people continually comment on how "strange" it is to work with expats.

Locals say that expats are *"Pushy."* Expats say that locals are *"Slow."*

For my purposes, I refer to "expats" as people from foreign countries who come to live and work here in Myanmar. Their situations may not be permanent; they have not rejected the values of their countries. When I use the term "expat," I am referring to someone who came here as part of a business or an organization.

## WHEN STRANGERS WORK WITH STRANGERS

Sometimes, issues rise to such a catastrophic level that expats leave Myanmar after only a month or so, citing the difficulties of adapting to the local scene.

Dealing with cultural challenges is one of the most daunting factors for expats all over the world. According to a survey of senior executives from 68 countries, around 90% see "cross-cultural leadership" as the biggest management challenge of this century. Up to 40% of managers sent on overseas assignments terminate early. The cost to employers of each early return is between USD 250,000 – 1,250,000. In most cases, the reason is cultural issues rather than professional, technical skills. Thus, the term "Cultural Intelligence" is emerging these days. The more globalized the world economy, the more critical cultural intelligence becomes.

The cultural challenge for expats is even more crucial in Myanmar. Since Myanmar just opened up, after over 60 years in isolation, it is unique compared with other Asian countries.

When they first came here, many expats experienced culture shock. Most of the time their first priority is to lower their expectations of the performance of the local workforce.

Similarly, local people are surprised when working with expats. Often they are confused about what they can do to meet the expats' (often their managers') expectations in their work. Sometimes local colleagues quit if they feel too pressured or stressed. It is not a myth that Myanmar locals do not confront conflicts head-on. In fact, they quit their jobs and report a different reason for doing so.

Culture shock for expats is far from rare in Myanmar. The expats are pushy – they came here because they have international and professional work experience and know how to get things done. They are used to managing people according to strategies, plans, goals, processes, deadlines, and so on. It is hard to imagine them not "pushing" to achieve business or organizational targets. The locals, on the other hand, are slow, for they have just woken up after years of being disconnected from the world. They were living in a dark period of history; they suffered from an outdated education system, and they lack adequate international and professional work experience. Things are just getting started here, and in ways unknown to them before. It is thus hard to imagine them not being "slow".

How can a baby run as fast as a trained athlete?

## WHY NOT A BOOK ON *"HOW TO SUCCEED IN MYANMAR"* FOR EXPATRIATES?

Having experienced culture shock, many expats in Myanmar seek resources on corporate working culture and the cultural conflicts between expats and their local colleagues.

A German journalist friend told me he was unable to find books or online resources on the topic. All the books he has seen on Myanmar culture fail to mention it, or only do so briefly. The few online articles about the business culture in Myanmar are very brief. There is only information about the general differences between the West and the East.

To my friend's surprise, I was lucky enough to have some specific experience on it, thanks to my working here in Myanmar in HR service for six years. Finding my perspective handy, and knowing I am a writer, he encouraged me to write a book about it. In fact, I am interested in interactions between global and local factors, and I did a master's degree in globalization and communication in England ten years ago.

That was the start of this book.

## A SURVEY ABOUT CULTURAL CONFLICTS IN THE GOLDEN LAND

To gain knowledge beyond my own knowledge and perspectives, I did a survey, asking both expats and local colleagues about the cultural issues/conflicts they often experience in Myanmar. Further, I asked what expats could do to improve the situation.

For the survey, I chose more than a hundred expats who have lived in Myanmar over a year. Plus, I had many in-depth discussions with expats who have lived here longer, some for six years, nine years, twenty years, or more.

Most crucially, I conducted the survey with fifty local professionals who have expats in their organizations – more than half of them are HR heads of sizable companies. They have had the experience of working with expats in Myanmar for years. Some have worked with expats for ten years, eighteen years, or even up to twenty-eight years. In-depth discussions helped me understand the local perspective more deeply.

Both expats and local professionals are from various kinds of organizations: international, joint venture, and local. Most of them are from companies, but a few are from NGOs or government organizations.

This book is full of vivid, real-life stories, mostly collected from the 30 in-depth discussions I had with locals and expats. The majority of the stories are from local professionals and expats, and some are from my own experiences in Myanmar.

### "MEN ARE FROM MARS AND WOMEN ARE FROM VENUS"

The outcomes of the survey remind me of the book *Men Are from Mars, Women Are from Venus.*

Through many generations, the relationship between men

and women remains challenging to both sides. They are "strangers meeting with strangers". The connection is fruitful only when they have a good understanding of the other side's needs and are able to respond to them adequately. Only with proper mutual understanding, seeing things from the other's perspective, is empathy gained.

My survey reveals to me that expat/local relationships are also built upon similar factors – respect, mutual understanding, trust, and acceptance. Then cultural integration is possible.

## WHAT TO EXPECT FROM THIS BOOK?
### Understanding the locals and the Two Survival Rules

This book embarks on its mission to help expats work successfully here first by furnishing an understanding of local behaviours in Myanmar. This includes in general social contact and in the corporate work environment. All the stories are real. People's names, of course, are changed.

To provide more in-depth comprehension of local behaviours, the book delves deeper by making linkages with Myanmar culture, traditions, beliefs, and religions. It does not exclude myths about the newly open country.

From the outcomes of the above survey, the book reveals the most common cultural issues for expats and their local colleagues in Myanmar and draws invaluable lessons. Expats "dodge bullets" in Myanmar rather than "bite the bullet" in numerous painful ways due to not "locking and loading" well!

*The two most significant rules for social interactions in Myanmar are demystified.* Expats, particularly from the West, can be lucid about the many annoyances and quirks they find here. This book aims to provide lenses to observe and comprehend the oddities, rather than leaving the expat to probe them with an unaided eye.

"Mind Your Steps" provides prescriptions for not offending locals, especially their religion and culture, e.g., "Never point your feet toward people" and "Shouting is totally unacceptable."

Notably, the book presents *15 common divergences between expats and local*s. For example, expats think locals are being dishonest when they promise to do something they do not comprehend, whereas locals think they are respecting seniors by not challenging them with questions.

### What locals think of foreigners: what I wish I knew before arriving here

It is said: "Learning from your mistakes is smart. Learning from the mistakes of others is wise."

The book responds to the very intriguing questions of expats: "What do locals think about foreigners?" and "Why do they think that way?"

What if you are extremely angry about a failed assignment because it seems to you that your local colleague should be able to do it with ease? The local colleague already said "Yes" when you two discussed it, and you felt assured about the outcome. Now your local colleague has resigned after your tirade. In fact, he felt threatened by your red face and shouting. What now?

Crucially, the book explores things expats should know before their arrival in Myanmar. Knowing those hundreds of cultural-specific oddities will save lots of time, effort, and money. Otherwise, any expat will make the same mistakes other expats have made and will have to "reinvent the wheel" to fix them.

### Three keys to succeed and 12 simple lessons

The sayings *"Success is no accident"* and *"Preparation is the key to success"* are unquestionably true in Myanmar.

Culture shock can be turned to our advantage. Professor Geert Hofstede - the leading scholar in intercultural theories defines culture as "the software of the mind." Understanding a culture as one would understand software like Dos or Unix or Windows can help expats multiply their productivity and achievements within that culture.

If every morning you wake up depressed and worn out about working in a land of myriad obstacles and oddities, now is the time to forge dramatic change. Understanding the local culture, then mastering thoroughly how to communicate with local colleagues – how to construct smooth relationships with them, and how to work with them to achieve your goals – are the cornerstones of your success here.

Myanmar is an exception to any previous corporate

experience an expat may have. *Three critical chapters of the book equip expats about how to succeed in the workplace in Myanmar.* They include how to communicate with locals adeptly, both verbally and non-verbally; how to build good relationships with them (a must); and how to work with them in Myanmar's peculiar context.

*Twelve simple and applicable lessons* can be "secret weapons" for those coming here hoping to rack up achievements.

**How to fix the damage done and suggestions to win**
The last chapter of the book stresses how to solve problems and repair any damage done. No one wants to offend local colleagues, but if there is damage, is it reparable? If so, then how?

Suggestions to Win are furnished, whether the reader is a two-year contract expat or a more long-term one.

Employing the "secret weapons", expats will go through an attitude adjustment; their relationships with the locals will enjoy fascinating alterations, and overall expatriates will find their burdens lessened.

When meeting with other expats in the "expat ghetto," you will not make a fuss about your frustration, as is all too common. Rather, every other expat will be infatuated with you. They all will desire to toast you with a glass of beer because you are a new role model who infuses them with fresh exuberance and knows the firm truth about working with local colleagues.

You will find yourself genuinely enjoying living and working here!

## Real-life stories and simple, applicable lessons for super-occupied expats

The book is full of authentic examples and stories. At the end of each chapter, applicable lessons are crystallized from key points as action steps. It is composed in a simple and applicable fashion. Change is possible for those who want it!

I know you may be someone who does not even have enough time for breakfast, lunch, or dinner. Sometimes you may forget a date or a call with your spouse! You may strive to have a meal in your car on the way to meet a client while sitting in gridlocked traffic. You feel you do not have enough time to sleep on the weekends, even if that is the only thing you want to do. Some can only read a few pages of this book at a time. That's fine. Picking up one item and practicing it will help, although going through the book from beginning to end can render better aid.

Even though the book does not aim at handing over a quick fix, there are simple and applicable suggestions for expats to apply. I believe you will start reaping the results of your efforts right away.

By the way, if you are reading the book and burst out, "Yes, that's exactly what happened to me!" then you will know you are not alone in Myanmar!

## *WHO THE BOOK WILL BENEFIT*

New expats and entrepreneurs coming here to work

Existing expats and entrepreneurs who want to improve their effectiveness and efficiency

Expatriates and investors who want to come to Myanmar or who are considering doing so

Travelers who want to have a deeper understanding about the people in the Golden Land

Local entrepreneurs and professionals who often work with expats, especially HR professionals

Anyone who is interested in gaining an understanding about Myanmar culture, business, and people in the transition period of connecting with the global world.

*For inquiries about the book, please email*
*hanabui.mm@gmail.com.*

# CHAPTER 1

# THE BUDDHIST COUNTRY AND THE TWO SURVIVAL RULES

## 1.1 A DEVOUT BUDDHIST COUNTRY

Religion is not always an alluring topic, particularly for bustling expats. But sometimes, knowing a simple equation in math can help an artist, such as a designer, earn more. Then he can take a rest to relax and create the works he really wants to do.

A Western expat said that his local colleagues were very amazed by and fond of him because he knows what an important role Karma plays in daily life here; he knows about the man-eating spirits in rivers and mountains, and he can guess which day of the week a local person was born from the person's name. It takes him less than 10 minutes, and 10 minutes is all it will take you to assimilate the content below.

It is inconceivable to understand the Myanmar people without a basic comprehension of their religion, specifically Buddhism, which is followed by 88% of the population.

## THE LOCAL PRIDE AND THE NEVER-FAIL-TO-ENCHANT PAGODAS AND TEMPLES

Nowadays, visitors to Myanmar are still captivated by the men wearing long skirts (longyi). They are also stunned by the pagodas, temples, and monasteries dotting the country. The unforgettable pagodas include those originally built in the time that Buddha lived; i.e., Sule Pagoda and Shwedagon Pagoda were constructed about 2,600 years ago. Notably, the magnificent Shwedagon is one of the most valuable pagodas in South East Asia. Local pride includes the world's biggest reclining pagoda in Mawlamyine, the longest wooden bridge in Mandalay, and so on.

Coming to Bagan – a must-see destination – visitors are often astounded by the thousands of very ancient and beautiful pagodas and temples whose charms will be indelibly imprinted in their memories, forever.

## BUDDHISM AS A WAY OF LIFE IN THE SAFE-TRAVELLING COUNTRY

Foreigners often feel they are very safe travelling here. Myanmar is one of the safest countries in South East Asia (as rated by Lonely Planet). It has a lower crime rate than other such countries. After nearly six years living here, I have rarely witnessed a quarrel, not to mention any violence. For a woman like me, travelling in Myanmar is very safe compared with other countries in the region. Of course, I do not go outside the restricted areas, and I use my common sense as any conscious traveler in the world should.

Buddhism, with its 5-precept practice, is one crucial factor that assures safety for visitors, plus the strict regulation of the government ensuring heavy punishment for harming foreigners. The 5 precepts of Sila Merits (Morality) are avoidance of killing living things, stealing, lying, sexual misconduct, and taking intoxicants.

King Anawrahta lived in the 11th century. He is one of the three most distinguished kings in Myanmar and is recognized as the father of the country. He established Buddhism as the main religion of Myanmar.

If you look at Myanmar's official holidays, 17 out of 28 days are Buddhism-related. Festivals are held almost every month here on the full moon. Everyone knows about the Water Festival (Thingyan) in April, and the Lighting Festival (Thadingyut) in October, but there are also Tabaung in March, Kasong in April, Waso in July, and Tazaungmone in November.

According to diverse sources, Myanmar is possibly the most devout country in South East Asia.

There are, of course, other religions, such as Muslim (4.3 % of the population) and Christian (6.2 % of the population), Hinduism (0.5%) and others (1.1%). Their followers are seen everywhere in Myanmar. Some places are more common for them than others, such as Rakhine State for

Muslims, and Chin State and Kachin State for Christians. The most notable religious conflict has been between Buddhists and Muslims.

In the early morning, if you go for exercise around Kandawgyi Lake in Yangon, people are doing exercises and bringing radios to listen to Dhamma talks (Buddha's teachings). Even when you go to local fitness centers, it is not uncommon to see people watching Dhamma talks on television programs on local channels. Dhamma talks are listened to in restaurants at various times each day. Dhamma talks shared by famous, reputable monks are also organized on residential streets on various occasions.

Buddhism appears in all the life-cycle events of a person's life, such as birthdays, novice ceremonies, weddings, funerals, and monthly and yearly festivals at which respected monks are invited to present and pray. On many streets of Yangon, there is a charity house to support donations to different pagodas and monasteries. People gather to do it. It is a good chance for socializing with your neighbours.

People worship both in pagodas and at home. From the early morning, local people have already come to pagodas to pray, offering and donating flowers, bananas, coconuts, money, and so on, to Buddha.

Indeed, Buddhism is interwoven in life here. Three-quarters of the people worship daily, and a similar proportion believes it is essential to follow traditions and establish values in their everyday life. This is according to a report of TNS Global.

## THE MOST GENEROUS COUNTRY IN THE WORLD - "CHARITY IS A WAY TO SUCCEED"

Donating to pagodas, monasteries, and to monks, nuns, etc. is one of the traditions here. Local people are very generous with their donations, even poor people. In the early morning, one sees many groups or individual monks and nuns going around local tea shops and restaurants in Yangon for alms. Restaurants often invite all of a group of twenty or more monks or nuns to have breakfast, all at the same time. They also put aside a separate big portion for donation, which they place in front of the restaurants.

In pagodas, the donation boxes are visibly full of bank notes.

There are local proverbs demonstrating people's mindset about charity: *"Charity is a way to succeed"* (Pay-kan-sunt-jeh-chin-ga aung-myin-chin-yet lan-za) or *"No charity, no wealth. No wealth, no charity"* (Ma-shi-lot ma-hlu ma-hlu-lot ma-shi). People believe that when we give anything, we feel gratitude towards the recipients because through them we are given the chance to do a good deed of Dhamma.

## "GENEROUS" IS NOT ONLY ABOUT DONATING BUT ALSO HELPING

Many friends of mine shared with me stories of being helped by local people who just had met them the first time.

If they asked local people for directions on the road, many times, they would bring the person there themselves to make sure he or she reached the right place. They do not mind that it costs ten or fifteen minutes of their time. On the bus, if you do not have the right change required for a ticket, people are willing to give you 200 MMK for it, easily. I have experienced this.

Further, when I go to local markets, people give me the same price they give to local customers, even though they recognize I am a foreigner.

According to the annual research of Charities Aid Foundations, which compiles the index of the most generous nations in the world, Myanmar in September 2017 was the most generous country for the fourth consecutive year. The annual survey covers more than 146,000 people in 139 countries. It measures the number giving cash, participating in volunteering, and helping strangers.

For most international visitors, Myanmar is a very hospitable country, and local people customarily give priority to guests.

### THE JOURNEY TO NIRVANA, KARMA, AND THE BELIEF UNDER THE FIRM DESIRE TO DO CHARITY

Though Myanmar is still one of the poorest countries in the world, Myanmar people are following Morality - the 5 precepts of Buddhism - rather than following money. Theravada Buddhism stresses spirituality, self–enlightenment, the importance of pure thoughts and deeds, and the importance of a simple life.

Buddhists want to reach Nirvana after their death – it is the ultimate goal to escape from the suffering cycle of life. They believe that they can be reincarnated after death if they have done enough good deeds. That belief is embedded in the Buddhist mind. (However, reaching Nirvana happens only for men. That is why men typically have a higher position than women in Myanmar. However, all the legal rights of women are equal to those of men, such as rights in ownership, inheritance, marriage, and divorce.)

The three requirements for Nirvana are Charity (Dhana), Morality (Sila), and Enlightenment (Bhavana), which involves insight, wisdom, and the cultivation of inherent good will and compassion.

Charity and good deeds are closely linked to Karma, a concept not easily understood by many Westerners. However, a Myanmar proverb says: "***Karma is the father and Karma is the mother***" (Kan-tha a-mi Kan-tha a-hpa). That is how important Karma is to life in Myanmar.

Buddhists accept the Law of Karma. Karma is believed to be the accumulation of meritorious deeds from one's previous life. It is not only limited to intentional actions but operates on the mental, verbal, and physical levels. Karma is accumulated by all kinds of thoughts, words, and deeds.

Karma is also used to explain the lives of people living in misery, such as beggars, prisoners, or orphans. It is believed that their situation is due to their bad Karma in a previous existence. This belief enables them to endure their hardships stoically. On the other hand, it motivates them to do more good deeds to influence their Karma so that their next life will be a good one, or at least a better one.

Why do people do so many good deeds in Myanmar? One crucial reason is that they want to meet the first requirement (Charity) to reach Nirvana in their next life.

### *WHAT HAPPENS WHEN YOUR LOCAL COLLEAGUES' HAIRSTYLES CHANGE TO RESEMBLE MONKS' OR NUNS'?*

Before Thingyan - the most significant festival here - many people customarily go to monasteries for a two-week period of meditation. The purpose is to purify themselves before the new year. During that time many people have their hair cut, since they will be going through a period of monasticism in the monasteries.

A Buddhist man becomes a monk at least once in his life. It is a way to bring good fortune or spiritual merit to his parents so that they will not descend to unhappy states of existence in their next lives. (Buddhism recognizes a kind of hell - a place of countless torments - but it is not eternal.) The ceremony of ordination is formally organized at monasteries. Supplicants will shave off their hair, wear the robe, and believe in Buddha.

Moreover, to reach enlightenment – one of the three requirements for achieving Nirvana – people also meditate.

Meditation centers are all over the country; there is even a kind of visa called a "Meditation Visa" for international visitors to Myanmar.

## 1.2 SUPERSTITION, ASTROLOGY, AND THE CRISPY U.S. DOLLAR

A local partner or a vital client suddenly invites you to go to Golden Rock for the attainment of good wishes. The person is highly enthusiastic. Will you go?

You will notice that your Myanmar partners or bosses sometimes may invite monks to their offices to pray – for long hours! In the meantime, you are waiting for them to make crucial decisions.

Your partner in real estate says a lot of things about avoiding places where man-eating creatures exist. They also insist on checking with astrologers about which day to begin construction. They will not start without consulting their astrologers. This is a crucial step for them. Will you follow them in this regard? Or will you more likely be exasperated at what you consider superstition?

Like any other Asian country, Myanmar is superstitious. Notably, women and people in rural areas are said to be more gullible than men and/or city dwellers.

In addition to belief in Karma in Buddhism, supernatural forces also fascinate the locals. They believe in psychic power. Psychic power can bring bad luck or good luck. Because of the effects of psychic power, people feel they need to follow specific rules to avoid danger and achieve success and happiness.

In the Myanmar language, the word "Nat" means "God." People pay respect and worship 37 worldly/spiritual nats. Nats can help people to achieve good things in life, but they can also create trouble for them if they fail to pay proper respect. In their previous lives, Nats were human beings with supernatural powers, but they encountered tragedy through sudden death. They were killed or encountered violence. The Nat Festival Tuangpyone takes place in August. It is very popular in Mandalay, with devotees from all over the country coming there to make donations and pay respects to Nats.

Many local people believe there are man-eating spirits in rivers, bridges, and railways. Places like rivers, lakes, mountains, and forests are thought by many to be inhabited by spirits. These spirits must not be offended. Local people particularly honor divine serpents (naga) that live at the bottom of rivers, lakes, and oceans. Some mountains, such as Mt. Kyai-hti-yo (Golden Rock) and Mt. Popa in the north are famous for having powerful spirits. Local people go there every year to pray that their wishes will come true. You should not wear red or black on these mountains because it would incur the disfavour of the spirits.

Regarding mythical creatures, white elephants are considered symbols of power and fertility. The white elephant is the most auspicious of all animals in Laos, Thailand, Burma, and Cambodia. In Yangon, you can see some white elephant statues at Kandawgyi Lake, near the Western Park Royal restaurant, when you enter from the gate in Bahan Road.

Moreover, animal guardians encircling pagodas is a familiar sight. Lions are considered the best guardians for religious shrines and edifices, since they are known for their bravery and magnificence. Other mythical images of creatures seen upon entering the famous Shwedagon pagoda are elephants, Nagas (dragon), Galon (Garuda), Hintha (Brahminy duck), and Kainara (birds with human heads and bodies).

### *WOULD YOU LIKE TO HAVE YOUR FATE CHECKED?*
I once did.

The astrologer in Sule Pagoda asked for my birth date and read my palm. After a careful checking with his thick and old books, he said boldly, "You were a Myanmar in your previous life."

Perhaps it is the reason why I have stayed here for six years and will continue to live here.

Astrology, palmistry, and clairvoyance still play a unique role in the lives of Myanmar people. This role is significant, as when people need to make decisions about marriage, business, naming babies, building houses and even political choices. Astrologers, fortune tellers, and palm readers can be found readily around the pagodas and temples. Some of them use English to communicate with and serve foreigners who are intrigued about their own destinies.

In many pagodas, symbolic animal statues stand, representing the eight birthdays in the week. People come before the relevant animals to pray. For example, a person born on a Tuesday will come to the Lion Statue. He or she will pour cups of water for the animal and Buddha. Usually, the number of water cups equals the person's age plus one. If a person is 30 years old, he will pour 30 cups into the animal and one to the Buddha statue. In downtown Yangon, Sule Pagoda and Shwedagon Pagoda are among the places for these activities and where you can donate for your own happiness and success.

**Birthday matches with Symbolic Animals**

| Birthday | Symbol |
|---|---|
| Sunday | Garuda |
| Monday | Tiger |
| Tuesday | Lion |
| Wednesday (am) | Elephant (with tusks) |
| Wednesday (pm) | Elephants (no tusks) |
| Thursday | Rat |
| Friday | Guinea pig |
| Saturday | Dragon |

Burmese astrology also associates a lucky stone, a direction, and a planet with each birthday. For marriages, there are some good days for couples and some bad days. The day the wedding takes place means either good or bad compatibility for the pair.

There are many auspicious or inauspicious days for doing things that people take very seriously. For example, if you build a house on a Sunday, you will be in trouble. For farmers, Monday, Wednesday, Thursday and Friday are good days for ploughing.

Critically, astrologers warn of possible danger, and they advise how to avoid it. Avoiding danger would involve following Yadaya – doing some good deeds to offset or delete the bad luck in the offing. Examples of good deeds would be mending a road, building a footbridge, freeing some fish, etc. In the turbulence of a shifting society, local people tend to believe more in astrology than before, as a way either to escape bad luck or to accept it if there is no remedy. Perhaps it gives a sense of having a measure of control over one's fate in a quickly changing world.

## THE CRISPY US DOLLAR

### How does the crispy US dollar connect to astrology in the Golden Land?

It is said that even the most high ranking generals or government officials are ardent believers in astrology, and they base their significant decisions on the advice of astrologers/fortune tellers. General Ne Win is notorious for his penchant for numerology. In 1987 he ordered all of the money denominations to be changed to 45 and 90 kyats, for he believed that 9 is a lucky number. Unluckily, many people's savings (sometimes their entire life's savings) were in old nominations, which disappeared. Numerous people went broke, and it was the beginning of a very dark phase in Myanmar history.

Consequently, expats and international visitors coming to Myanmar should only bring new, clean, and crispy 100 US dollar notes. This relates to the fact that local people keep their savings in US dollars (and gold) because of the instability of local currency.

## 1.3 SURVIVAL RULE 1

Myanmar is a hierarchical country as opposed to egalitarian Western countries. The Survival Rule 1 is Hierarchy.

### HIERARCHY (YA-DO-GONE-THEIN A-HSINT) OF THE FIVE FOREMOST RESPECTED ONES

As noted previously, Myanmar is a very devout country; therefore, norms and traditions here customarily are associated with Buddhism, the religion of nearly 90% of the population.

These are the five foremost respected entities: Buddha, Dhamma, Sangha (Community), Parents, and Teachers. "The three gems" (three venerables) are Buddha, Dhamma, and Sangha together.

Buddhists show utmost respect to Buddha. Images, paintings, and statues of Buddha represent him and therefore also must

14

be respected. When entering a pagoda, people are requested to take off their shoes and socks and to dress respectfully: no revealing clothes. As a pagoda is a holy place, they are expected not to make noise or do rude things.

People show respect to monks, nuns, and novices (even if they are children). Non-monks are expected to sit lower than monks. A woman should not touch a monk. Practically, international visitors are advised not to touch a monk's robe.

### Don't disrespect the Buddha – the vital law

Such cases as the following hardly ever occur but should be taken into consideration. Similar to the King in Thailand, Buddhism and religion command great respect in Myanmar. Articles 295 and 295(a) of the Myanmar Penal Code prescribe up to four years' imprisonment for "insulting religion" and "hurting religious feelings." Authorities will use these laws against foreigners if they are found to be using the image of the Buddha disrespectfully.

Jason Polley and Cesar Hernan Valdez - both Canadian - were expelled from Myanmar on their respective trips in 2014 and 2016 because of their perceived disrespectful behaviour toward the Buddha. They had tattoos of Buddha on their legs, which locals viewed as an insult to their religion.

The case of Philip Blackwood (New Zealand) stunned the expat community in Myanmar in 2015. He was sentenced to two years in prison due to using a Buddha image in his advertisement pamphlet for the V Gastro bar. The image of

Buddha looked as if he were drunk. Four local lawyers refused to defend his case, possibly because it is such a sensitive matter here.

A list of Dos and Don'ts in Myanmar appears in the Appendix. It is officially recommended by the authorities to international visitors (and thus expats) who sojourn in Myanmar.

The next priority after the three gems is the Parents. The family is critical to a Burmese. Knowing a person means knowing his family status. Children are expected to pay respect to their parents and follow their advice (or orders). A family has an impact on its members' actions. For example, if parents do not want their children to work in sectors concerning alcohol or cigarettes, the children agree and obey. There are many cases of students studying medicine because their parents want them to. (By the way, doctors are highly regarded in Myanmar society.)

Teachers are in the fifth position in rank. It is believed that in school, students should listen to their teachers. "Teachers are always right; don't ask questions" is the belief. This kind of obedience is compatible with the study method of "Repeated learning" in schools and universities (rote learning) when students try to memorize and repeat what teachers tell them. They are not encouraged to ask teachers questions, to think on their own, to have new ideas, or the like.

Nowadays, with the fantastic communication revolution and affordable internet access in Myanmar, many people are taking online courses, but the traditional education method is still prevalent in public education.

## THE SOCIAL HIERARCHY OF "PAYING RESPECT TO ELDERS OR SENIORS"

Elders and seniors are highly regarded in Myanmar society. For example, at meals, people do not eat until the oldest one starts eating. In a meeting in an organization, a younger person may not dare to express an opposing idea to an elder person or his manager. It would be considered inappropriate. As such, a younger manager may face some difficulties managing her older subordinates.

Many foreigners say they do not understand why there is such respect given to elder colleagues, without any particular reason. There is indeed a reason – age links to wisdom and knowledge. As a local proverb puts it: "*The older the person, the wiser his brain.*" (Shar bin o-lay a-hnit pyit-lay)

Understanding the social custom of paying respect to seniors is essential for people in an organization in Myanmar. For example, a junior does not dare to "ask back" a question to a senior. That would be considered challenging a senior, which violates the hierarchy. In fact, a very habitual behavior of local colleagues in Myanmar is to hesitate to "ask back" an expat supervisor. Even if they do not understand what is being said, it would violate the hierarchy of respect for them to seek clarification and understanding by questioning the person.

Titles associated with rank are crucial, as well. For example, a director is higher than a manager, so many people would prefer a job with the title of director rather than manager. There may not be much difference in the job scope and salary. The pay might even be lower, but the title would make up for it in status, and thus they would prefer to have the director title above other considerations.

## THE BODY HIERARCHY

*On a beautiful morning, John was eager to go to the office.*

*His team was achieving better business results than expected. He came to the office earlier than usual, enjoying the fresh air on the way when he walked from the parking lot to his office room. Feeling good, John was singing his favourite song, "Beautiful Sunday", though it was just Friday.*

*When Hlaing came to say good morning to him, John saw a strange expression on her face. She usually was cheerful and polite. Now she looked as if she were asking: "What the hell are you doing?"*

*Confused, John self-consciously checked himself. He was here in this room, the proper place at the right time, his new shoes were shined, and his clothes were perfect with the white linen shirt, the red tie, and the grey trousers. He was always careful in his dress, for his appearance was important in his position.*

*Then he noticed that the table was shaking under his feet because he was so excited, and his singing made him want to dance.*

*Oh, my goodness – I put my feet on the table! John realized with a start. He had broken a taboo.*

## The holy and the impure body parts

In Myanmar, it is important to be aware of your head and feet. The head is considered holy – it is the most sacred part of the human body – while the feet are considered impure. The feet are the lowest part of the body; they are beneath all the other parts of the body and touch the ground and many nasty things (i.e., dirt, mud, rubbish, etc.).

As such, it is advisable not to touch anyone's head, and it is strictly forbidden to point at things or people with the feet.

It is not only at pagodas that people are requested to take off their shoes. Sometimes they are requested to do so in offices and homes as well. If you visit someone's house, you should do so.

For many foreigners, especially Westerners, putting their feet on the table is normal. However, for local people, it is bizarre and rude! You should not touch objects with your feet either, such as nudging an object aside with your foot. There is nothing more insulting to a local than your pointing feet towards him or her. They may not say it to you, but that is what they think.

It is even worse if you point your feet at an image of Buddha. So you should tuck your feet under yourself when sitting on the floor or ground.

It is advisable that you hand things over and receive them

with your right hand, as a courtesy gesture. Support the right arm with your left hand while handing over things.

### THE GENDER HIERARCHY

In Myanmar, men are often considered superior to women.

In a family, the man (husband, father) is the highest person, the owner of the family. Women are housewives, taking care of daily household matters and arranging domestic affairs such as cooking, washing, cleaning, or childcare. The men are breadwinners and thus hold the right to decide on essential matters such as the family's house, land, car, job, education, etc.

Similarly, sons usually possess higher positions in families than daughters. This is especially true in Buddhist families, because they will re-incarnate in the next life while women cannot. The novice ceremony for a son would be a great source of pride for a family! Women are sometimes not allowed to enter some areas of a pagoda.

### THE POLITICAL HIERARCHY

Hierarchy is also found in the government-civil relationship. For example, in meeting with government, companies' representatives are expected to be patient and subject to possible postponement by the government officers, who may have more urgent matters pressing upon them. Offending government officers is to be avoided entirely. For example, it is important not to push too much or demand too much.

## 1.4 SURVIVAL RULE 2

The Survival Rule 2 is Anadeh (incl. Saving Face)

*ANADEH - A PERVASIVE NUANCE OF BURMESE CULTURE*

It is eye-opening to many foreigners, especially Westerners, to see how important "**Anadeh**" is in Myanmar culture. Anadeh strongly shapes social interactions in Myanmar. People follow Anadeh, even at the expense of honesty, efficiency, or their own interest.

"Anadeh" is a broad term, and it is hard to find an equivalent translation in English. It is a kind of behavioural philosophy underpinning daily interactions of people here. At the core of Anadeh is the desire to create and nurture positive relationships with other people.

"Anadeh" would be primarily interpreted as "consideration". It means not wanting to offend others by disappointing them, or causing them to "Lose Face", or making them feel uncomfortable. There is always hesitation or equivocation about doing something that would lead to such consequences. Thus, local people usually would feel on edge about disappointing anyone, in one way or another. They will say what they think you want to hear rather than voicing their opinion.

Habitually, Myanmar people try to "respect" others - to be gentle, courteous, and considerate. For example, if on the street, they bump into you by accident, they say, "Respect," ("ga-dot" in the Burmese language) very sincerely. "Respect" here is stronger than "Sorry". It means the offense was not intentional and they still respect you, so please be sympathetic.

Anadeh includes **Saving Face** for others and oneself. Blunt criticism of someone would be regarded as rude. It would cause that person to "Lose Face". For example, in a restaurant, a person would not return a dish of bad quality because of Anadeh. A subordinate does not want to voice his own opinion, because it may differ from his manager's and cause the manager to "Lose Face".

Anadeh also reflects the avoidance of conflict. Anadeh is operating in a background of Buddhism, which values harmony in the family and community and focuses on the cultivation of goodwill and compassion. Hence, the consideration of Anadeh is very appropriate in situations where one's interests might conflict with others'.

For example, a father will keep his bad debt secret so as to keep his children from being agitated about it. A guest may say he is not hungry because he is fearful that the host will expend time and effort to prepare food for him. A manager does not point at someone or name the person directly who made a mistake at work, though everyone knows who it is.

### A SIGNIFICANT SOURCE OF MISUNDERSTANDING BETWEEN EXPATS AND LOCALS

Anadeh is similar to "Kreng Jai" in Thailand, which is considered to be "the essence" of Thai-ness.

Kreng Jai still bewilders lots of foreigners there, though millions of foreigners have lived in Thailand for decades. Kreng Jai's simplest interpretation is also "consideration" of others - being respectful, polite, and considerate to them. A Thai colleague may not want to point out your error in a meeting because he feels "Kreng Jai" toward you; he wants to be respectful.

Obviously, Anadeh would make it hard for people to express their honest thoughts or give frank feedback. A local colleague, then, will not say "No" to or confront an expat. It would violate the "Anadeh" rule.

Thus, even when local colleagues are unable to do a job, they do not want to say "No" to expats. When they say "Yes", it may very well mean "No". Expats, in such cases, think that local colleagues are not honest, or that they do not deliver on their promises.

The truth is, local colleagues do not want to offend you by saying no. They think it will disappoint you! Indeed, they think they are doing a good thing by saying yes when the answer is really no.

Anadeh is the explanation for the avoidance of conflicts and confrontation in the working environment, too. People do not want to cause stress or make other people uneasy. Since they have a strong sense of consideration for others' feelings, and they do not want to bring to others the pressure that conflicts and confrontation bring.

From my survey of over a hundred expats, "Avoidance of confrontation" is one of the most common cultural conflicts in Myanmar between expats and locals. When local colleagues have conflicts with their managers, for example, they resign from jobs without revealing the real reason rather than sit down to discuss and resolve the conflicts.

Let's go into a little more detail about how Anadeh includes "Saving Face".

### SAVING FACE – A SURVIVAL TOOL

The concept of "Saving Face" (Myet-hna a-hpat-hseh) belongs to Anadeh of Myanmar, although it is typical in Asian countries. The face is equal to one's honor, reputation, influence or dignity. Thus by showing respect to someone, or by complimenting him, you are giving him "Face" (Myet-hna). On the opposite side, criticizing or blaming someone, especially in front of others, would make that person "Lose Face" (Myet-hna pyet).

To "Save Face" for people, communication needs to be indirect. Directness would be considered rude. For example, "No" is not a polite word. If one does not agree with something, one would say, "I will think about it," or "Maybe," or "I am not sure" to be polite in Myanmar.

One expat from America, who has worked here over four years, sums it up: *"Don't mention that someone made a mistake. Don't correct people. Don't argue."* All are related to the "Saving Face" rule. People are vulnerable, and they react negatively to criticism.

There are cases when expats shout at their subordinates (local colleagues). The worst negative consequences may follow. Local colleagues will feel offended and resign if they are shouted at. Even when they receive a good salary, they will resign. For them, it is not about how high a salary they get, but about how well they are treated.

Again, Face is a significant underpinning of society that is "more important than truth or justice." That is to say, Losing Face is a tremendous fear. Losing Face would threaten the individual's relationships in his or her community and is arduous to get back once lost. Making others Lose Face, then, is to be avoided at all costs!

Why is Face of that much significance? It is because collective values play a pivotal role in Asian societies. This is very different from the individualistic values of the West. The focus in Asia is more about fitting in the community than standing out personally. People's actions are influenced by such thoughts as: *"What will other people think if I do it?"* or *"Is that acceptable to other people?"* or *"Is my behaviour like others'?"* This puts many things at "Face" value.

As parts of a devout country, Myanmar people's communities are often monasteries. For life-cycle events such as birthdays, wedding, funerals, etc., people often invite monks to come to pray for them to receive good fortune and do good deeds. Monks are sought out for advice in life as well. "Monastery education" is one of the education channels in Myanmar. It is unique in that it allows poor students to procure an education without having to pay tuition fees.

Teashops are places for people in a community to meet and stay connected. People sit in crowded teashops on every corner of Yangon, meeting, discussing things or entertaining themselves.

Communities are the network around their companies, their bosses, colleagues, and subordinates.

Surrounded by neighbourhood communities, people know that "bad news" about them can spread very quickly, so they are very much afraid of "Losing Face". How can they meet and look their acquaintances in the eye if their "Face" is smashed?

## 1.5 THE SUBTLE INDIRECTNESS REQUIRED

The Two Survival Rules in Myanmar indicate that subtle indirectness is desirable. The rules are not explicitly spoken or written out, but if one does not follow, the consequences would be obvious. The Hierarchy rule requires that one understand who and what are priorities and therefore must be respected. The Anadeh rule requires one not to offend others by being inconsiderate of their feelings or situations.

*One day was particularly memorable for many employees of a major local business group. It was not only so because it was the day of an annual meeting for senior management executives. It was memorable because of an uncommon event.*

*The expat General Manager (GM) had been in Myanmar for over a year and was in charge of business development for a dynamic business branch of the group. The assignment required him to make various changes in the organization to boost the business and achieve the target. He had been seen as a hard-working senior who always returned home very late after office hours, i.e., 7 p.m., 8 p.m. Indeed, it was a hard job for him, as it would have been for anyone in his shoes.*

*It took a long time to get him into this position in Myanmar. The company owner had selected him as an outstanding candidate among multiple ones who were introduced by famous headhunters from Singapore. He, of course, had extraordinary experience in the field with a proven track record of success in his career in business development. The owner had to make a very tempting offer to bring him in to realize one of the group's ambitions.*

*The meeting went slowly and stressfully. The GM needed to achieve much, with too little support. Even knowing that patience is a must for working in Myanmar, this Asian expat found it hard to bear it all anymore. He burst out shouting at the group CEO – a local executive.*

*"I cannot understand why it is not possible! You promised me before that you would hire more people, including expats. Now it is exactly the opposite! What can I do with all the out-of-date people you have here? How can I reach our extremely high target? Can you tell me, please?"*

*The group CEO who was being shouted at said nothing and*

*stepped out of the room.*

*Shouting at his senior, in front of other colleagues, cost the expat a lot. He was forced to voluntarily resign, for the CEO later said to others: "If he does not resign, I will."*

Myanmar people habitually communicate softly and politely. It relates to the habit of avoiding conflicts and confrontation in the name of Anadeh. Consideration for others' feelings or situations is assumed, and people go out of their way not to offend.

Indirectness is commonly seen in Asian countries. However, in Myanmar indirectness is required by their ethic of the "gentle manner", even more so than in China, Korea, Vietnam, and so on. The Burmese people are, generally speaking, very gentle in social interactions. Being too direct, assertive, or aggressive is considered rude.

There is a local proverb, "***A wise man never reveals his anger***" (Pyi-nya-shi a-myet a-pyin ma-htwet).

Repression of anger could seem strange to many foreigners, who are used to showing their emotions spontaneously. In Myanmar, if an expat shows his annoyance or strong negative emotions, local colleagues are very sensitive to it, and they do not respond positively. They may make more mistakes.

In fact, they are scared!

Looking back on the story example, if an expat shouts, he creates a very negative image for himself. In doing so, the expat violated the two survival rules – Hierarchy and Anadeh. He was not only being disrespectful to his senior; he was also smashing his senior's Face in front of his subordinates.

An HR Director for a reputable international hotel with twenty-two years working with expats, both overseas and in Myanmar, stresses: "**Shouting is totally unacceptable here!**"

Keep calm in all circumstances, please!

# CHAPTER 2

# THE TRAUMATIC HISTORY
# AND THE INNER INSECURITY

## 2.1 THE RECENT TRAUMATIC HISTORY AND ITS CONSEQUENCES

A first-time traveler to Myanmar nowadays would still be enthralled by the men wearing long skirts (longyi) and eating red-colored betel. It looks like a very traditional society from the outside.

Further, they would be shocked by the under-developed side of the country – the electricity goes off many times on some days, clean water is a concern, the health care system is still very modest, etc.

Some funny stories of foreigners travelling around the country have been shared with me. When I was in Pyay some months ago, a couple from Holland was thrilled to meet me, as I am a fluent English speaker. They had only been a week in Myanmar (they had not been to Yangon or Mandalay yet, where there are more English speakers).

What was most appealing about their sharing was, however,

that while they were here for the local attractions, they found themselves to be the attractions to the locals! They were tall, white, with blond hair and blue eyes – all are visible even from a distance. There were similar stories of Western guys in Myeik as well.

Not many foreigners have been to Myanmar, in contrast to other neighboring countries such as Thailand, China or India. If local people see them, they often stare at them with curiosity and ask in a friendly way: "*Where are you from?*" if there is a chance to strike up a conversation.

Yes, Myanmar was closed and in isolation for over 60 years, passing many dark decades of history.

At the moment, life is still a daily battle for survival for most of the local people.

Looking back to the 19th century, three Anglo – Burmese Wars took place between 1824-1886. The colonial period was from 1886-1948, when Burma was under British rule. Then, there was co-operation but later conflict with the Japanese till May 1945. Subsequently, Burma gained independence from the British on January 4th, 1948 under General Aung San's leadership. After that came the socialist period (1962-1988), government by military junta (1988-2011), a semi-civilian government (2011-2015), and most recently, the NLD democratic civilian government of Daw Aung San Suu Kyi. In 1989, Burma was re-named Myanmar.

Ethnically, Myanmar society is a diverse one. 135 ethnic

groups are living in Myanmar. The Burmese account for 68% of the population. Because of this, Burmese is the official language of Myanmar. Though Burmese is a common term referring to all people in Myanmar, each ethnicity has their own cultural identity. The other largest ethnic groups are the Shan, Kayin (Karen), Rakhine, Chin, Kachin, Mon, and Kayah. In addition, there are Chinese, Indian, and Rohingya people.

During each historical stage, there were many alterations in Myanmar society. There were many military coups. Thus, whatever their ethnicity, people's lives have been, to some extent, unstable. Indeed, the Myanmar people have seen much historical trauma. When one includes the civil wars in the country, Myanmar has experienced 236 years of conflict, or about 40% of all those experienced in South East Asia. The country has sustained 30% of all conflict casualties. The Karen rebellion, starting in 1949, is the longest in modern world history, though there have been ceasefire agreements between the central government and the minority armies.

The consequences are that nowadays about one half of the population lives below or at the poverty line, according to the World Bank's definition of that. Health care is among the worst in the world; the education system is outdated. Myanmar is one of the world's poorest countries with an annual income per capita of 1,300 USD/person (World Bank figures, 2017).

Ironically, it is a place where wealth and opulence co-exist and contrast with vast poverty. A small percentage of the population lives in wealth. They are the elite.

In 2008, the Cyclone Nargis widened the gap between the rich and the poor here, further adding to the plight of the poor. It killed about 138,000 people, with over 190-km winds and a 3.5-meter tidal surge in the Irrawaddy Delta area. Over 2,500,000 people were affected, and many lost their homes. The economy was impacted because the affected area is the rice bowl of the state, producing 65% of the state's rice, 50% of its poultry, and 40% of its pigs.

The country faces other issues that spill over to its neighboring countries such as refugees, minorities, dissidents, and others.

These factors unquestionably have had an impact on the characteristics of the Myanmar people. The environment in which people dwell conditions them somewhat. Since the turn of the century, Myanmar has been through different episodes of history and politics. That much fluctuation has had an effect on the people's psychological make-up.

## 2.2 THE INNER INSECURITY

Expats or international visitors might feel that many local people are too shy, not outspoken, and sometimes not confident. At the same time, it is clear that the people are extremely courteous, friendly, hospitable, helpful, caring, and patient.

## DIVERGENT GENERATIONS

Ko Maung is a repat in the advertising sector. He was employed overseas in South East Asia for over ten years. He remarks that the Myanmar people all have different characteristics, but they share one thing in common.

It is their inner insecurity.

In his postings, he talks a lot about the psychological characteristics of Myanmar consumers, which he categorizes into different generations. His opinion sheds some light on the case.

Generation Y, those born between 1980 – 1994, is the most significant part of the current local workforce. They are, at the moment, in the age range of 25-39 years old. This is a questioning generation who are always asking themselves: "*Who am I?*"

## THE REPRESSION PERIOD AND THE INNER INSECURITY OF THE WORKING FORCE

Generation X (born 1965 - 1979) went through the darkest period of their lives between 1988 – 2010. The Myanmar people were most suppressed during that time. Myanmar was one of the most censorship-controlled countries at that time, ranking 164th in lack of freedom out of 168 countries.

After 1988, Myanmar faced a very uncertain future: internal war, inflation, and corruption after 26 years of the socialist reign of General Ne Win. The inflation breakout in 1988 devalued the local currency to a significant extent and made many people's entire savings disappear in just a few days!

In those days the junta government did not allow public expressions of opinions about its problems and was highly sensitive to opposing views. Censorship of all publications and media, including imported books, was in full force. Orthodoxy alone was considered valid. To criticize the government or to hold views other than the approved dogma meant the person would end up in jail or experience some other kind of trauma. The authoritarian military regime spied on its employees and citizens, harassed political activists, intimidated, arrested, detained, and physically abused all dissidents.

Political rights were entirely restricted. There were no rights of assembly or association. Workers' rights were repressed as well, and unions were banned. People's every action and communication were monitored. It was common for the government to employ forced labour for public works and in order to produce food, goods, and services for the military. Even people's assets, like their homes or their money, were subject to confiscation without compensation.

Ko Maung's life story is a witness to the traumatic history. He was imprisoned for distributing printed material written by a student political party. Ironically, at that time the junta government claimed to be democratic. His whole family tried to save him from prison by activating their various connections with the police. He would have spent many years in prison if not for help from his uncle. His uncle had a good relationship with the military station captain, whose wife was his ex-student.

Fear was rampant then. The period is remembered by many Myanmar as a terrifying time.

Then, the Saffron Revolution, spearheaded by the demonstrations of Buddhist monks in the fall of 2007, was brutally suppressed. It reminded people of another notable previous suppression: in 1962, the military fired on some 2,000 students who were protesting, killing perhaps as many as 100. The military only admitted to killing 15. The Rangoon University Student Union was blown up.

Generation Y lost their hope for a bright future and always asked themselves: "*What should we do?*" Many became teachers; many became real estate brokers, and many went overseas for better jobs, including seamen jobs. There are successful Burmese expatriates overseas, i.e., in Singapore, Thailand, Malaysia, Dubai, Australia, UK, the U.S., and elsewhere. They work as professionals; they are accountants, engineers, hoteliers, doctors, lawyers, entrepreneurs, etc. Many of them have returned to Myanmar since the country opened in 2011. They are called "repats" in this book. They nonetheless constitute a modest portion of Generation Y.

Some people in Generation Y were able to overcome the challenges and be successful. They became entrepreneurs, journalists, media people, photographers, etc. But a more significant number of them have failed. The gap between successful and failed people of this generation is sizable: unsuccessful people are far more numerous than successful people. Many felt bitter, frustrated, and hopeless. Thus complaining, blaming, and fighting occurred frequently among themselves and in their families. Many found themselves turning to membership in gangs. Hope died in many of them.

Thus, most people of Generation Y feel insecure inside. Outwardly, this manifests in a lack of confidence and assertiveness.

The website 16personalities.com provides references about the MBTI index of people in various countries based on surveys. The surveys found that Myanmar people are slightly more introverted, observant, feeling, introspective, and turbulent than people in other Asian countries.

The comments of many expats about the Myanmar people's characteristics echo the results of this survey. The traits "slightly more introspective and turbulent" also resonate with the above comment of Ko Maung on the inner insecurity of Myanmar people. It is hard for them to be assertive in life; they do not know where to position themselves for success in such an ever-changing society!

The younger generation, those who were born since 1995, are more hopeful than other living generations in Myanmar. Those under 30 years old, especially those under

23, learn new things more swiftly and are not afraid to put what they learn to use. They are dynamic and energetic. That is the observation of a European expat who has lived in Myanmar for over 12 years.

However, according to Ko Maung, the very young are disconnected from older people and the traditional culture. They wear Western clothes, play hip-hop music, and use the internet very actively in both work and entertainment.

They are good at catching up with the digital trends, but maybe not so good at keeping up with the past.

### A HIGH UNCERTAINTY AVOIDANCE

Many expats think that local colleagues are afraid to try new things. They do not want to take initiative, and they resist change. Adventurousness and willingness to take risks are much lower than in neighboring countries, according to the survey. What's more, in many cases, because people feel insecure inside, they hide things, which makes expats think they are not sincere or honest.

Myanmar's current culture is one where avoidance of uncertainty is high. According to "An Exploratory Study of Myanmar Culture using Hofstede's Value Dimensions" that Charles Rarick and others conducted in 2006, Myanmar's people score high in avoiding uncertainty. Myanmar scored nearly 90 points in this area, whereas Malaysia, Philippines, Indonesia, Singapore, and Thailand scored 38 points, 45 points, 48 points, 8 points, and 64 points, respectively.

Myanmar's people are closest to Thailand's people in terms of uncertainty avoidance and farthest away from Singaporeans.

## 2.3 THE SELF FROM READING THE NAMES

It is said that one's own name is the sweetest of words to anyone. Myanmar names tell a lot about the person.

Local colleagues say, *"Wow!!!"* and are very glad if an expat can explain the meaning of their names. Further, learning to understand Myanmar names will provide you with hints and insights into your local colleagues' personalities. You will be unquestionably equipped with that knowledge soon! Read on.

To begin with, how do you address a person in Myanmar? In Myanmar, people's names are not divided into parts like the given name and family name. The whole name is a given name. There is no family name. Thus, the name reflects things about the individual person.

### *THE HONORIFICS*
Honorifics should be placed in front of names to indicate age, status or rank, as below. It is a way to show respect.

|  | Male | Female |
|---|---|---|
| Working adult, typically older than you | U (actually means uncle) | Daw (actually means aunt) |
| Working adult | Ko (older brother ) | Ma (older sister) |
| Young people | Maung (younger brother) | Ma (older sister) |

39

| Teacher or boss | Saya (male teacher) | Sayama (female teacher) |
|---|---|---|
| Head/Senior Teacher or Big boss | Saya Kyi (senior male teacher) | Sayama Kyi (senior female teacher) |

### *NAMING AFTER THE BIRTHDAY*

A person's name in Myanmar is constituted of different factors. Birth date and ethnicity are commonly indicated. From his or her birthday, a person's personality can be derived.

The following table will show how names relate to birthdays of the week and the possible personality traits associated with each.

| Birthday | Symbol | Names start with | Possible Characteristics |
|---|---|---|---|
| Sunday | Garuda | A, E, I, O, U Ohn, Aye, Ee, Aung | Too sensitive (if the person has curly hair, he or she is not too sensitive). Selfless, and is loved by everyone. Positive and motivational, a challenge-taker. |
| Monday | Tiger | K, Kh, G, Gh, Ng Kyaw, Khin, Kyin, Kyi, Ngwe | Organized, sometimes jealous. Smart, alert, and a lot of attention to detail. |

| Tuesday | Lion | S, Sh, Z, Hz, Ny San, Sann, Sue, Soe, Nyi, Nyein, Zaw | Stubborn. Natural leaders who fight for what they believe. |
|---|---|---|---|
| Wednesday (am) | Elephant (with tusks) | W, L Lin, Win | Quick temper. A little unpredictable. Put 100% effort into tasks. Vibrant and can inspire excitement in others. |
| Wednesday (pm) | Elephants (no tusks) | Y, J | Quick temper (mild). Introverts, careful and calculated in everything one does. |
| Thursday | Rat | P, Ph, B, Bh, M May, Ba, Mya, Myat, Maung, Myint, Myo, Min, Moe | Harbours grievances. Adaptable, good problem solver. |
| Friday | Guinea pig | Th, H Than, Thant, Thein, Thaung, Thinn, Thaw, Han | Very talkative. Excitable and creative. Emphatic. |
| Saturday | Dragon | T, Ht, D, Dh, N Tin, Tun, Nu, new | Hot temper. Fiery, social but sometimes self-isolating. |

**Source:** *(Meiji Soe, 2017), (Saw Myat Yin, 2011), (Taylor, n.d)*

As a result, if a person has the name Lwin Lwin Htun (commonly a female name), then local people would guess she was born on a Wednesday morning because it starts with "L".

Each name would have other meanings according to each word in it. For example, there are many names containing "Aung" which means "Win or Victory". For example, U Than Aung, Dr. Myint Aung, Daw Aye Aye Aung.

Hnin Phyu means Snow White (Hnin – snow, Phyu – white). Phyo Pye means Completely Happy (Phyo – happy, Pye – complete). Nay Soe means Big Sky (Nay – sky, Soe – big).

### NAMING AFTER THE ETHNIC ORIGINS

As noted previously, there are also names revealing ethnic honorifics.

|  | Male | Female |
|---|---|---|
| Shan royalty | Sao (Saw in written) | Sao (Saw in written) |
| Shan | Sai | Nang |
| Kayin | Saw | Nan |
| Mon | Mahn, Mehm or Nai | Mi |
| Kachin ruler | Duwa | (no female equivalent) |

**Source**: *(Saw Myat Yin, 2011)*

If a person's name is Saw Hla Chit, it is possible he is a Kayin ethnic. People would call him U Saw Hla Chit - this is a bit of repetition of honorifics, because U and Saw have the same meaning. Further, Hla means beautiful in Burmese. Chit means Love.

So, the person is a beautiful love!

## 2.4 AVOIDANCE OF BAD NEWS AND CONFRONTATION

*A logistics expat manager shares that when there was a new regulation issued by the government about the customs clearance procedure, she was not informed in time.*

*The new rule would cause difficulties for the logistic service company as it meant they had to take more time and money to follow it. Unaware of the new rule, the manager did not have the application checked. The goods failed to be labeled in the new way the government required.*

*Thus, the containers were delayed at the port while the company paid out more money to fix the issue. Clients complained about the lateness of the service, too.*

*It was a mistake, the manager told her local colleagues, that should not be made again. However, she did not reveal whose mistake it was.*

No doubt someone wanted to avoid giving her the bad news of the new, onerous regulations. This reticence cost the company time and money.

What scares expats is that together with avoiding reporting "bad news" like this, local colleagues also typically try to avoid possible confrontations. The following is a case in point.

*An ASEAN Finance expat manager was thinking that his financial analyst was chatting too much with friends over the phone in the office in Burmese. He was not happy about it.*

*Actually, she was trying to chase down local clients to register vendors' information into their new system. They were reluctant to provide so much information to the company, some of which was sensitive or had not been requested before.*

*Further, she had to work with joint venture staff comprised of government officers. She had no authority over them. She could not give them orders, impose deadlines, or hold them accountable for their promises.*

*What was more, the international company's procedures were complicated. She needed to answer many questions from different reporting lines from the office in Singapore to other offices in Australia and Europe.*

*She was overworked, with an intense workload. However, wishing to avoid confrontation, she did not report all the difficulties to her manager.*

It was only after the lady resigned and some time had passed that the expat understood all the things she had been doing. She was not chatting with friends over the phone at all. The expat had not understood the woman's job well enough to protect her, even in relation to the regional office. This lack of protection troubled the lady.

Unfortunately, by the time the manager realized his mistake, the lady had resigned.

These stories are examples of Myanmar people tending to avoid giving bad news and confrontation.

In my survey addressing more than a hundred expats, they say that a "different attitude towards conflicts" is one of the three most widespread cultural conflicts they encounter here.

Because the tendency of local people is to avoid telling the boss any bad news, many expats are angry when they get bad news too late, after it has become harder to fix things. Yet even under normal conditions, many local colleagues already are scared or try to hide from expats if they feel their English is not good enough, let alone when bad news happens.

It is the result of the inner insecurity, plus Hierarchy and Anadeh (including Saving Face) rules.

### DON'T TAKE THE FIRE OUT OF YOUR HOUSE

Instead of reporting all the difficulties in their jobs and "confronting" their manager to discuss possible solutions, local colleagues try to do everything themselves. Local colleagues try to tackle the difficulty since the manager thinks they can do it. They do not want to appear to be incompetent. Or they ask themselves: *"Is it too small to report to the manager?"* *"I don't want to burden my manager, do I?"* *"Is it better I solve the problem first?"* *"Will I lose face reporting it to the manager?"* or *"How can I report it properly when my English is poor?"*

According to a managing director of a local reputable consulting firm, there is a Myanmar saying: *"Don't take the fire out of your house."* It means there is usually no open discussion about bad news because it is not polite and they might lose face with many people.

Aside from the cultural pervasiveness of age-old traditional rules, people still feel cautious due to the repression period (1962 – 2011). Openly discussing bad news or having different views from the higher management (government) levels was forbidden and severely punished.

The insecure self inside many Myanmar people contributes to approaching commerce and business with too much fear. Local colleagues are sometimes riddled with fearful feelings, and it causes them to hesitate when they should go forward. Remembering the tragic history and trauma of Myanmar can help expats understand why local colleagues behave as they do. It can also help expats take effective and empathetic measures to gently encourage their local colleagues to come forward with more confidence.

## CHAPTER 3

# INEXPERIENCE VS. INTERNATIONAL STANDARDS, AND THE WORKING RELATIONSHIP

### 3.1 WE ARE ALL FAMILY

Listening to conversations in Burmese, many times one hears the words "A Ko", "A Ma", "A Daw", "U Lay", "Ta mi", "Ta". These are all family relationships: they mean "brother", "sister", "aunt", "uncle", "daughter", and "son", respectively. It is the custom here to refer to strangers as family members!

In markets, teashops or in restaurants, an elderly seller calls a young female customer "Ta mi" or "daughter". The same seller would call a young male customer "Ta" or son.

In the West, an older man may call a young man or boy "son", especially when the older man is in a paternal position and is giving advice or help, i.e., a teacher, coach or policeman. However, family relationships are not embedded in the culture as they are in Myanmar. Even when dealing with each other on the job, Myanmar people use family terms.

A Myanmar proverb: ***Preference is given where the blood is thick*** (A-ye-ji-hlyin thwe-ni-thi).

A comparable Western saying is: "Blood is thicker than water", meaning that blood relations will get preferential treatment over non-relatives. Indeed, family-style business culture is still customary in Myanmar. Many employers recruit employees because they are relatives, friends, or acquaintances of the business owners or senior managers. People are rewarded with jobs due to their loyalty and conscientiousness, not because they are capable.

It was only in 1998 that Foreign Direct Investment was allowed in Myanmar. In 2012, nearly a year after the U Thein Sein government declared reform in April of 2011, America and the European Union began lifting their economic embargoes on Myanmar to open doors for investors from those countries.

Before the opening of Myanmar in 2011, there is even not much competition among businesses. There was a number of local, major business groups who together accounted for a considerable portion of the economy. They were, indubitably, operating like family-style businesses.

The family-style business culture also requires an introduction from a trusted local person if you want to build up business relationships quickly. A German consultant who has worked for some years with both the government and the private development sectors calls it, "a saya-based culture."

According to him, an introduction is needed by a "Saya" (teacher, boss, or senior) for quicker establishment of connections or relationships. For example, if someone wants to meet a minister or general director in a ministry, it is optimal to be introduced to him by one of his acquaintances, such as an ex-classmate, an ex-teacher, an ex-colleague, etc. Someone may still meet with local people without being introduced, but the encounter would be more formal and less sincere.

Facebook is an excellent channel to get in contact with a local, even for business purposes. When locals want to connect with someone, they often ask if the person has a Facebook account. Using Facebook will help you build relationships, if you are not afraid of revealing your posts to your business partners or local colleagues. A very high-ranking government officer (i.e., a minister) previously disseminated news to the media via Facebook. People in Myanmar are not accustomed to using Google Search, but they use Facebook intently, i.e., on a daily basis.

A general director of an Italian construction material company with over three years' experience working here suggests that convivial meetings are best organized around meals, such as lunches and dinners at restaurants, not at offices. He mainly works with government officers and local businesses.

Connected to the family-style business culture, a friendly and relaxed working atmosphere prevails. A local designer, who has worked with expats over six years, was talking about his boss, a European expat:

*"He is so strict! Whenever I am late for work by only 10 minutes, he seems unhappy. For deadlines, he always wants me to submit all the required layouts on time.*

*But I am an artist, and sometimes I need more time for creativity. Why must everything be precise? I wish he would please relax more!"*

*"Expats are so rational and unfriendly."*

Locals think foreigners are too strict about deadlines, reporting or task details. "*Too rational, no feelings – they only focus on the job!*" they say.

## 3.2 WHEN THE HEART WINS THE MIND - RELATIONSHIP IS KEY IN THE FEMININE CULTURE

The majority of over fifty local professionals answering my survey cited **"relationships and communication"** as key issues for expats here.

An accountant in an international company spoke about her direct manager – an expat:

*My boss – the Chief Finance Officer – is not kind at all, although he is very professional and smart, with lots of international experience.*

*Even when I have a fever and am coughing, he ignores it and continues to give me tough tasks with tight deadlines. For example, he requires a detailed fixed asset report to be submitted the same day!*

*He is very cold and does not know about my personal situation. How long does it take me to office from my home? More than an hour, sometimes two hours due to the problematic traffic in Yangon. He rarely asks me about my family, my ethnicity, my home. He does not know my difficulties on the job, and my dream to be a professional chief accountant one day.*

*There is no caring at all.*

*Maybe he looks down at me ... I do not like him very much.*

*We do not have a good relationship. I am just barely surviving but not very happy with my current job. I am looking around for another job if there is a chance.*

## THE FEMININE CULTURE AND THE SUCCESSFUL WORKPLACE

A survey by Alana Rudkin and Joseph Erba in 2014, based on Hofstede's cultural dimensions, showed that Myanmar has a feminine culture. It also suggested that a successful workplace in Myanmar is based on building personal relationships, establishing mutual trust, and celebrating group achievements.

A feminine culture values feminine characteristics such as co-operation and caring over achieving goals. It emphasizes happiness over competition.

According to Hofstede, a masculine culture presents a preference in society for achievement, heroism, assertiveness, and material rewards for success. Such a society at large is more competitive. Meanwhile, a feminine culture prefers cooperation, modesty, caring for the weak, and enhancing the quality of life. Such a society is more consensus-oriented.

In the business context masculinity versus femininity is **"task orientation"** versus **"person-orientation".**

As mentioned before, Geert Hofstede developed a model of the four dimensions of a culture, namely: power distance, uncertainty avoidance, individualism vs. collectivism, and masculinity vs. femininity.

The original model of Hofstede was the outcome of factor analysis done through a global survey of employees' values at IBM between the years 1967 and 1973. Hofstede's work established the base for other research in intercultural psychology. This theory quantified cultural differences, scoring each country in each cultural dimension.

For example, Thailand scores 34 on femininity and is thus a feminine society. Thailand has the lowest masculinity ranking among the average Asian countries (53) and the world average (50). This indicates a less assertive and competitive society.

Expats in Myanmar experience Myanmar locals as *"emotional and welcoming"* rather than *"rational and distant".* Local colleagues in Myanmar often welcome expats thanks to their friendly nature. They are emotionally driven, and building rapport with them is a prerequisite for expats to work successfully here.

In this scenario, expats would be viewed as *"cold"* or *"too rational"* if they do not pay attention to building good personal relationships with their local colleagues or not taking personal factors into account.

When locals see expats devoting themselves to work but not caring for people, they think expats are too ambitious and selfish, and that they only know about work! It makes them look like *"like robots"* without human sensibilities.

For many Myanmar people, it is hard to separate professional matters and personal matters.

*"Emotionally, Myanmar people react based on their feelings and how they are treated,"* a local manager for a European Financial Service firm comments.

Likewise, one finance repat from Singapore who has logged over 15 years working with foreigners both overseas and in Myanmar comments:

*"People here are soft and emotional. Sometimes, Anadeh makes them feel 'sorry' too much whenever they make a mistake, or when they are facing a problem. So making them feel comfortable is 'a must'.*

*Many people do not care about the employment contract. Only the 'heart contract' makes them follow you.*

*It depends on if people like you or not whether they follow your leadership."*

This echoes a Myanmar proverb – ***"If one hates, he finds faults. If one loves, he finds excuses"*** (Chit-hlyin a-joe mone-hlyin a-pyit).

## 3.3 WHO CAN MOVE THINGS AND THE POWER DISTANCE

***TRANSFORMATION OF GIANTS ON THE WAY***

The de facto question is: "Who has the decision-making power in organizations in Myanmar?"

*A famous hotel in Yangon was struggling to find executives and senior managers.*

*They wanted to recruit various expat professional managers for the hotel. Nonetheless, when some professionals came to work, they called it quits not long after starting their role, i.e., after one week, a month, or a few months.*

*They often did not know how to navigate and lead their functional department (or even the whole organization) when having two decision-making bosses at the same time. The owner is the father, and the other owner is the son, who was given the authority to control the hotel. However, the father was still involved in the operation and made different decisions than the son.*

*How can an organization move forward having two divergent directions at the same time?*

This section is more relevant to local companies and organizations where the family business model is dominant than to international companies. A number of notable local companies, under the new pressure of current competition, are trying to modernize their organizations by hiring expats to re-build their business strategies and re-structure their organizations. At the same time, they are hoping to reap the full advantages of doing business in an open international environment.

To understand those business giants' background, it is important to remember that normally wealthy major business groups here must have close relationships with the military government, in particular with senior generals, to build up their business empires. First, they get licenses for extracting natural resources such as gems, jade, teak wood, minerals, metals, etc. and then use the money gained to invest in other business sectors such as property, hotels, media, banking, trading, telecom, etc. The connection with the generals and military government are their most crucial business advantages, and there was not much market competition before Myanmar opened in 2011.

Those giant companies are bringing in lots of expats for their transformation. Moving giants, however, takes lots of time and determination. Many expats working for local companies (usually only big ones can afford their remuneration packages) find out that they may be not suitable to work in family-style organizations, even in huge companies. Delegation does not work, because the decisions are mostly still made by the business owner. In some cases, senior managers can also make decisions, but it is not always the case.

A British expat who has lived here for over three years comments, *"The thing is that the most imperative person is absent many times, and while he or she is unwilling to delegate decision-making to lower managers, the critical decisions are left pending for many days and weeks."* Thus, it slows down the organization's operation. Many expats find that they cannot meet the owner's requirements, such as meeting business targets, as they do not have enough authority to make things move.

There are many stories like that in Myanmar, when a local company wants to restructure the organization up to international standards by hiring expats. It is understandable and reasonable during transitional times, though, that the strategy, the organizational structure, and the business plans are not clear yet, and the rules and regulations of a company are not yet systematically established. That means it is hard to allocate decision-making to anyone but the company owner.

The power distance is considerable in Myanmar - the above stories illustrate that. It is also physically reflected in the different chairs in a work room or meeting room. The biggest chairs are for the more senior people; others are similar, but smaller, and these are used by the rest of the gathering.

For local private companies, in most cases, the family owner makes all the decisions or delegates it in a very limited way to top management. Thus, if you arrange meetings with them, it is advisable that you research to find out if the person you intend to meet has enough decision-making power for the matters at hand. Otherwise, the meetings may be fruitless.

**Summary – Implications for expats who want to work for local corporations**

|  | Expats | Locals |
|---|---|---|
|  | Be aware of the family-style business operation about decision-making and delegation. Prepare to be confused. Prepare to be impatient due to prolonged waiting for decisions | Business owners often make all decisions. May send others who cannot make decisions to meetings. May delay making decisions |
| Solutions | Expats research to find out who the decision-makers are and other factors that would contribute to the decision-making process | |
| Solutions (long-term) | Accept that things are what they are and that changes will be very slow. See if one is able to fit in that environment and be patient enough | |

## 3.4 THE ELASTIC SENSE OF TIME

An Asian expat shared about his experience of meeting a potential Myanmar business partner:

*The appointment was at 12 p.m. I arrived on time and tried to call the person at 12:15 p.m. when he did not show up, but I could not reach him.*

*Then at 12:30 p.m. the person rang me up to say politely that he was on the way.*

*We met at about 1 p.m., and we were very excited.*

*The local spent the whole afternoon with me.*

It is not rare for many people to be late in Myanmar, and they do not dare to inform you they will be late. In many cases, people accept that it is okay to be late by about 30 minutes. They may even be late "forever" (which means they do not show up at all). The reason usually given is that their lateness is due to a bad traffic jam.

"*Time is money*" is a well-known proverb.

It is true in Myanmar, too, but in a peculiar way. Myanmar people typically do not run after money aggressively. Rather, their craving is to follow the five precepts of Buddhism. They are also very generous with their money in countless ways. The proverb is valid because local people are very kind-hearted with their time too, as well as being benevolent with their money.

Many expats or travelers to Myanmar share that local people are not afraid of giving time-consuming help to others. An example would be showing directions to a foreigner by escorting the person to the place to make sure the foreigners reach it, even if this takes 10 or 15 minutes.

Myanmar people are willing to donate their time to a mere stranger.

I experienced this many times. I was sometimes hesitant to receive their help, but they were never reluctant to give it. For example, whenever I stopped passersby or passengers to ask the meaning of Burmese words on a signboard on the road, people were always willing to help out, very enthusiastically.

Nonetheless, it is not accurate to assume people will invariably be late for meetings. My friend, who works in a service agency, said that her senior local candidates always come on time to meetings she has with them. Also, people who are used to working in international companies have better habits when it comes to being exactly on time for meetings.

Many expats are concerned about a lack of urgency about deadlines in Myanmar. While expats think that locals are "*slow*", locals think that expats are *too* "*pushing*". The "*relaxed manner*" in Myanmar might lead a local colleague to fail to meet a deadline for a task, especially when they are handling various assignments at once.

The gap in attitudes toward time is deeply rooted in the feminine culture of Myanmar, which prioritizes harmony and relationships over achievements.

## 3.5 THE SCARCITY OF INTERNATIONAL EXPOSURE AND A LONG LIST OF MISSING SKILLS

The requirements of foreign companies for locals in order for them to be up to international standards are far removed from the skills sets of locals. As mentioned before, due to the recent history of Foreign Direct Investment in Myanmar, lots of things are new to the local workforce, including international standards of professionalism. The normal expectations of expats, based on international standards, are well beyond their local colleagues' experience, education, and imaginations.

*ANALYTICAL SKILL AND THE INADEQUACY OF*

*EXPRESSING ONESELF*

To get the whole picture of something, expats often need to ask local colleagues a series of questions, digging around to get to the truth. The conversation below would be an example.

*Why do you not want to do this job?*
*Because I do not like it.*
*Why do you not like it?*
*Because it is a marketing job.*
*Why you do not like a marketing job?*
*Because I have to go around to sell products.*
*Why do not you not want to go around and sell products?*
*Because I am afraid people do not want to talk to me.*

Instead of saying outright, "I do not like this job because it is a marketing job, and I have to go around to sell products to people who may not want to talk to me," the person answers with a single piece of information unconnected to the broader foundation of his or her thinking on the subject. The expat has to extract enough information to make the links by asking leading questions.

One ASEAN expat with two years' experience working in Myanmar commented that: *"Local colleagues do not normally fully express themselves."* He works in general management in the industrial sector.

Another conversation might go like the one below. The context is an expat arranging for a junior candidate to meet an interviewer.

*Can you meet Mr. Lukas on Thursday at 3 p.m. or Friday at 10 a.m.?*
*I am sorry. I am not available then.*
*When is a good time for you to meet him?*
*Can I meet him Friday at 2 p.m.?*
*He is engaged then. What times are usually good for you to meet? Can you give me two or three options?*
*Then I usually would do it after working hours. Or on Saturday.*

In the above example, a question is asked, providing two different options, and the local's reply is simple, limiting options. The local does not voluntarily come up with other options. The expat needs to continue asking different questions again and again to work something out.

When choosing employees for work in Myanmar, international companies do well to give priority to those who have analytical skills. Many HR local professionals say that people with this skill are rare in Myanmar.

## *THE CONTEMPORARY MODEST LEVEL OF ENGLISH SKILLS*

The heyday of English as a foreign language is long gone in Myanmar. However, the English skills of many high-ranking government officers and business leaders here are great, as many expats find out. In the colonial period under British rule, English use was very widespread. What is more, in the late 1950s and early 1960s, Myanmar was one of the wealthiest countries in Asia. Rangoon University became one of the most prestigious universities in South East Asia and one of the top universities in Asia, attracting students from across the region, i.e., from Japan and India. That is why the English skills of the above people are amazing - they can communicate directly with foreigners.

Yet the present Myanmar workforce, in general, does not possess excellent English skills. Of course, many working people can use English well, but not the majority of them. Sometimes people speak English well, but their writing skills are not as good. This is due to the out-of-date education system. Students learn English in school, but the focus is on passing examinations, not on practicing the language. Further, the history of the usage of English by local people while working with foreigners is not a long one yet.

## THE MENTAL BLOCK

Local colleagues who "think outside the box" are considered desirable by expats, for many expats to think that local colleagues do not take initiative, relying instead on tried-and-true experience or their supervisors' instructions.

The Anadeh (including Saving Face) and Hierarchy traditions already cause Myanmar people to "contemplate" things many times over before formulating or disclosing their positions on a matter. This is so as not to offend or embarrass others or themselves, and not to be rude to seniors or elders.

The backward education system is also to blame. While Myanmar once had a good, reputable education system, today it is criticized for teaching methods which emphasize repetition and memorization, without questioning things, and thus gaining knowledge without real understanding.

Crucially, the censorship of the junta military and its top-down management also silenced many people. In the past, people were deathly scared to discuss things like politics publicly. These days, even though the political scene has shifted, people are still hesitant to offer their opinions on different matters. Being vigilant has become a survival habit!

All this has happened in the context of nearly 60 years of traumatic isolation, with limited access to the outside world.

Therefore, many local people seem to possess a kind of "mental block" which manifests as being too shy to utter their thoughts or to dare to try new ideas.

## PERSONALITY AND FAVOURITE JOBS

There are certain jobs that by their nature are not easily filled in Myanmar.

Sales and marketing jobs are undesirable, for many people associate them with "Going around everywhere trying to sell things". With Buddhists, insisting that other people do things they may not be interested in doing violates "Anadeh". Further, the Myanmar people have a tendency to be "introverted" (as per the research outcome of the 16typesofpersonalities.com). Jobs that require meeting lots of people are generally avoided.

There is a considerable database of local accountants or IT guys. Working with numbers and computers rather than with people are suitable occupations for "introverted" people. Getting accounting certificates and degrees for the sake of getting a job is very popular in Myanmar. If you are recruiting, it is not uncommon to find candidates with LCCI (accounting) degrees, even though they are not applying for jobs in finance or in the accounting department.

As shared in Chapter 2, many Burmese who went overseas for jobs consider returning home nowadays, or they have already come back to work as repats. In Singapore, according to a reputable recruitment agency, Myanmar people normally do three jobs while there: accounting and finance, engineers (IT, mechanical, petroleum, etc.), and domestic helpers.

Interestingly, many companies in Malaysia and Singapore hire Myanmar people for such money-related and sensitive roles as cashiers or money keepers. They believe Burmese do not know how to steal! Burmese are famous there for being honest.

## THE LONG LIST OF MISSING SKILLS AND THE TALENT GOLD RUSH

One European HR head of a local business group, with six years working in Myanmar, comments: *"They need everything here."* The list of skills local colleagues are missing is long. It is the result of decades in isolation and jeopardy.

The missing skills, according to the man quoted above, as well as many HR Heads of international and major local companies, are: English, IT basic (Excel, Word), Communications, Critical Thinking, Creative Thinking, Problem Solving, Time Management, Leadership, Teamwork, Presentation, and others.

The Talent Gold Rush started in about 2015 – 2016, when Foreign Direct Investment was flowing strongly into Myanmar. The local workforce is not ready yet; thus, the local shortage of skilled talent makes for a big gap between demand and supply.

Salaries for professionals are thus on the way up. According to a reputable recruitment agency, many international companies find that in Myanmar they need to increase their salary budget, while the requirements for the job have to be decreased.

The consequences are that many international companies see their employees jump from job to job quickly (job hoppers), especially the ones with good English skills. Whenever they switch to a new company, they normally get a higher salary and a better position. The salary offer is often 20 – 30 % higher; it may even rise to 50% higher, or it may even double. Thus, they change jobs every 6 months or year. They are hunted by recruitment agencies and companies to fill many new vacancies.

### *THE PREVIOUS BRAIN DRAIN AND CURRENT RETURNING TO HOME COUNTRY*

For many international companies, "repats" are desirable. (Employees with years of working for international companies are also considered desirable.) With prior experience working overseas, repats are both international and local and thus adjust easily to working with expats. Nowadays, with many local major groups re-engineering their businesses, headhunters are after repats.

As referred to in Chapter 2, there was dark period of history in Myanmar. Generation Y (born 1980 – 1994) faced the most challenging historical period. Trying to answer the questions *"Who am I?"* and *"What should I do?"* they do not have much hope in the local job market. Many of them accepted the challenge of working overseas to support their families. They went to Thailand (especially people who lived near the Thailand border), as well as Malaysia, Singapore, Dubai, the UK, the U.S., Australia, etc.

It is estimated that more than a million Myanmar people are working in Thailand. Many live and work in the north, i.e, Chiangmai, Chiangrai in the tourism sector. In Singapore, there are more than 200,000 Burmese.

These days many repats are returning to Myanmar because of the good opportunities here. The local workforce too is getting more experienced after some years of interacting with international companies. In the context of the currently less aggressive Foreign Direct Investment into Myanmar, the pressure on recruitment has gradually lessened.

# CHAPTER 4

# WHAT DO LOCALS THINK OF FOREIGNERS? MIND YOUR STEPS

## 4.1 WHAT LOCALS THINK OF FOREIGNERS

*HOW DO WE KNOW WHAT WE BELIEVE WE KNOW?*

In his famous book *How Real Is Real*, philosopher Dr. Paul Watzlawick debated about the connection between communication and reality (which is a relatively new idea). He put it: *"How do we know what we believe we know?"*

Indeed, how can we justify our knowledge about the world that we "know"? There are many assumptions underlying our thoughts, without our being aware of it. They include stereotypes, prejudices, and other generalizations.

Likewise, in Myanmar, local people observe foreigners from their own perspectives, which are rooted in their values, beliefs, memories, customs, metaprograms, and more. As mentioned, Myanmar people usually are inquisitive about foreigners, for there are not many foreigners in Myanmar yet. This is especially true compared to other countries in the region like Thailand, Malaysia, Vietnam, etc. Foreigners are stared at as they walk across local streets in Myanmar.

Local people apparently have mixed views about foreigners, depending on who they are and what their goals are in interacting with foreigners. For example, a business that once enjoyed a monopoly would perceive foreign businesses as threats, while a small or medium business would think foreigners might lead to new business opportunities. A local employee might believe foreigners bring better jobs, but are strict and demanding. Junior locals may think that expats are always right, while a repat may think that expats want to bully locals and are only here for the money.

Expats may be astounded to realize how locals observe them and what they conclude about them.

## WHEN LOCAL PEOPLE THINK POSITIVELY ABOUT FOREIGNERS

### Some locals think:

Foreigners are experts.

Foreigners know many things – they have good knowledge, methods, and techniques.

Foreigners are good at strategy and management and are very internationally experienced.

Foreigners are advanced so I can learn a lot from them.

Whatever foreigners say is right.

Foreigners come from more developed countries than Myanmar.

Foreigners are rich.

Foreigners are bringing many new things to teach and help locals.

Foreigners bring finance and investment here.

There are currently better jobs than ever thanks to foreign companies.

There are more business opportunities in Myanmar thanks to foreigners.

Expats are more approachable than Myanmar bosses.

Foreigners are more straightforward than Myanmar people. Their subordinates can ask questions and negotiate. Foreigners are flexible.

Many foreigners are polite and know Myanmar culture.

Some foreigners take part in local festival events and other family events of locals, which is so lovely.

My foreigner boss is very caring, polite, and talented, and he inspires us a lot.

## WHEN LOCAL PEOPLE THINK NEGATIVELY ABOUT FOREIGNERS

### Some locals think:

Foreigners are strange. They do many things differently than we do.

Foreigners are too pushy. They want everything quickly, while in Myanmar things are slow.

Foreigners do not understand Myanmar, so they want impossible things.

Expats do not understand the reality in Myanmar - they only want to sit in the office and check emails.

Foreigners want things systematic and up to international standards while things are chaotic here.

Foreigners are threats to locals.

Foreigners come here for money only. Many of them are cheaters.

Foreigners' salary is very high. They demand a lot when it comes to apartments, cars, and other benefits.

Foreigners criticize Myanmar subordinates a lot.

Foreigners are very arrogant and look down on people.

I do not want to work with foreigners - they do not know the Burmese language, so they cannot do the operation.

Foreigners have good language and presentation skills only.

Foreigners bully locals who have less knowledge than they do and only use locals to take advantage of them.

Foreigners are customarily rude and abrasive.

Many foreigners have hot tempers and shout at other people.

Foreigners are very demanding, so working with them is very difficult.

I try to avoid talking with foreigners. I am scared. My English is not good enough.

Foreigners are not respectful to local people and culture, though they know the culture. They travel all the world and are knowledgeable. They just do not want to follow the "dos and don'ts."

Foreigners are cold. Not friendly at all!

They are not caring and not kind. They give me tasks when I am sick. They only want the result.

Foreigners get into groups and complain a lot about Myanmar. They do not mingle with local colleagues.

Foreigners use bad words such as "F*ck" or "Sh*t".

Foreigners are not sincere and do not want to train us. They only want to protect themselves during their working contract.

Foreigners are very strict. Deadline, reports, rules, etc. - everything needs to be accurate.

Western and Asian foreigners are different. Westerners are normally more democratic, while Asian expats normally show more power distance.

Foreigners never listen to local colleagues or ask for their opinions. They only want to give orders and do things their way.

## 4.2 HOW LOCAL EMPLOYEES SEE EXPATS

A local manager at a 4-star hotel has worked with expats for years. He thinks: *"My foreigner boss (Westerner, General Manager) is stingy! His salary is very high, and he does not need to pay for his own food. Yet for a taxi trip home, he tries to bargain from 2,000 MMK to 1,500 MMK! I am surprised."*

A local banker with over ten years experience working with expats says: *"Expats are much more knowledgeable and have advanced experience in modern banking. They come from the advanced countries, and they have advanced degrees. I try to learn from them as much as I can, in order to be professional and excel in my career."*

Sometimes local colleagues think expats are too cold. For example, expats share the expenses at meals. Many Myanmar people pay for their relatives or friends without a thought. Translated into a business meeting, that would mean one person would treat the rest. This is typical in many Asian cultures. A person who is richer may be willing to pay, or a person with more success than his companions may be willing to pay. An older friend may feel that he or she is like an "elder brother" or "elder sister" and may be willing to pay. By contrast, expats think it is not fair or that things are unclear if only one person pays.

One HR head of a petroleum company reflected: *"Expats usually get together in groups and complain about Myanmar."* She says they complain about everything from the hot weather to the cleanliness, to traffic jams, electricity, local staff members, the government, etc. That is her experience after working with expats for over ten years in Myanmar. She continues: *"I wonder, if all they say is true, why do they stay?"*

### A STORY ABOUT "MR. WHY"

A local professional has a nickname for his European country manager. It is "Mr. Why". Whenever "Mr. Why" encounters a setback, he asks "Why?" with annoyance and lots of complaints. *"Why is the internet is so slow"?* *"Why are people in the nearby coffee shop so noisy?" "Why is it so smelly in the meeting room?" "Why is it so noisy in my apartment in the morning?"* (8 a.m.), or *"Why doesn't the government reply to us quickly?"* So they change the internet provider, the office location, and other things to try to accommodate him, yet the complaints continue.

Local people think: *"This is Myanmar."* It is like in Thailand, when people say, *"TIT – This is Thailand."* They feel that the expat is too demanding about everything. Even if they have worked for a particular organization for several years, an insensitive expat supervisor can make them want to quit as soon as their annual contracts are up.

## A STORY ABOUT MR. "WHY IS IT NOT LIKE IT IS IN SINGAPORE?"

A story shared by an HR professional of a major local business group:

*My ex-boss is an expat who comes from Singapore, though he is originally from another Asian country. He is a General Manager in charge of business development for the group, which is transitioning from a family business to a more professional one. It seems he was shocked by Myanmar reality and the local workforce.*

*He constantly says things like: "In Singapore people are not like that," or "People here are lacking in skills and very weak in performance compared to Singapore," or "I need to hire more expats; local people cannot meet international standards like they can in Singapore." He sometimes says to candidates interviewed by the company: "How dare you apply for that role? Look at your ability." He never listens to local opinions.*

## A STORY ABOUT "MR. POLITE, FRIENDLY, AND CARING"

An HR head of a joint-venture financial service firm shared the following story.

*My boss is an Australian who is very polite, friendly, and caring. He is very patient and tries to understand others' opinions. He is also flexible, not as strict as other expats.*

*If there is a company party, he will go around the tables and does not just stick to one table with other expats. If we have problems in our jobs, he will ask, "What are your difficulties?" Also, he is interested in our lives and often asks us such questions as: "Where do you live? How many people are there in your family? Are you happy in your job? What are your career goals?"*

*Sometimes he attends family events or festivals, e.g., he will go to a wedding or attend a family funeral or Thadingyut Festival. He went to the stage performance of the festival. He also eats local food in the food court nearby.*

*We like him the best and are very willing to do our jobs under his leadership. We also want to help him if he has any problem in Myanmar. He respects us, and we respect him.*

## *A STORY ABOUT MR. NAÏVE*

Many local major business groups are hiring lots of expats to modernize their giant businesses. Usually, an expat is an expert in his or her field and typically has worked in international companies for years. That experience motivates the local owner to hire them to make use of the expats' global exposure.

*Yet the HR Manager of a local bank thinks that the expat banking experts in her bank are "naïve". She feels a bit funny when expats trustingly ask her if their roles are going to last long in Myanmar, because the bank often reports losses on their Profit & Loss statements.*

*They often know nothing more about the business group than what is on the official website, which never mentions the real function of the bank in the business group, or how the groups built themselves up to be giants. They do not know how the group gets its profits as a whole. Naïve expats also do not know about the links between the government and business owners.*

The major business groups have many businesses. In this case, the bank is used for their branding in modern industry, as well as being a financial tool for their other businesses, which include real estate, hotels, trading, mining, etc.

Usually, the business owner has good relations with crucial generals and through this has received licenses for extracting natural resources such as the mining of metal, precious stones, or teak wood. Then they use the cash obtained from that to invest in various other businesses - real estate, hotels, logistics, FMCG, airlines, banking, insurance, etc. (This was mentioned previously in Chapter 3, article 3.3).

*"To me, they are 'naïve expats',"* she concludes with a sparkling eye.

## 4.3 "I WISH I HAD KNOWN BEFORE ARRIVING HERE!" BEYOND THE DOS AND DON'TS

*"There is very little 'of course' when it comes to customs."* (Janet Kagan, *Star Trek – Uhura's Song*)

Local customs and characteristics of Myanmar seem abnormal to expats because they are very different from theirs. An expat who is used to overseas assignments, though, understands that there is nothing irregular here; it is just different from their experiences. The more assumptions they make, the more odd things will seem.

As noted in the preface, I reached out to more than a hundred expats who have/had worked for over one year in Myanmar. One of the questions they were asked is: *"What are the three things you wish you knew before coming here, but in fact, did not?"*

## "THE STRANGER SEES ONLY WHAT HE KNOWS" (AFRICAN PROVERB)

The things that expats wish they could have known before coming to Myanmar include things related to the missteps they made because they did not understand things in advance. The lists below include the answers that recur the most. You will note that many of the thoughts of expats are the same, yet some are contradictory to others. It depends on the person, his or her attitude and experience, and the situation they are or have been in.

In fact, philosopher Paul Watzlawick said: "*All perception and thought are relative, operating by comparison and contrast.*" (*Change: Principles of Problem Formation and Problem Resolution*)

### I WISH I KNEW IT BEFORE ARRIVING HERE

#### How and what locals think of foreigners

How they observe and come to conclusions about expats
What they think about expats

#### Local people's nature

People are very kind.

People follow the five precepts of Buddhism rather than money. They will quit high salary jobs if they are unhappy.

Religion is fundamental. It is a sensitive matter here.

People are superstitious and even invite monks to pray at the office.

Keep your distance; no touching. Especially do not touch people's heads or point at things with feet.

People are very calm and have a peaceful nature.

People are very honest, especially at local markets. They sell things to me at the same price charged to locals.

People are very helpful, especially when I ask for directions. They do not mind spending time helping me.

People are very polite and soft.

People are shy and humble.

People are very generous; they donate a lot even if they are poor. They give foreigners money for bus tickets when we do not have small change.

People are amiable and hardworking.

## Communications

Misunderstandings are common.

People say, "Yes" whether they mean it or not.

People cannot take being shouted or yelled at.

People say, "Yes" but they may not agree.

People say, "Yes" but may not do what they agreed to as they do not really understand, or are not capable of doing it.

People are too shy to say what they think or to ask questions. They are reluctant to offer opinions.

People hide and are not open about things.

I need to listen carefully to understand things.

Relationships with locals are significant.

To be introduced is very important in building up relationships with new people.

Bonds are significant prerequisites for business deals.

Face-to-face meetings are important (versus emails, phone calls).

Being diplomatic is important; frankness can be considered rude.

Speak softly. Raising your voice is viewed negatively.

## Hierarchy, Anadeh, and Saving Face

Saving Face is essential, especially when resolving conflicts.

Hierarchy is fundamental. Age is respected without reason. Seniority is everything.

Anadeh is very important.

Anadeh is difficult for Westerners to understand.

Anadeh sometimes means to avoid communicating/ reporting bad news.

## Working manners

People are relaxed while working.

People may not work well under heavy pressure.

Don't discuss work over lunch. People want some relaxation then.

People might not report terrible news when issues pop up. They try to avoid confrontation.

People don't find it easy to accept professional criticism. People may be reluctant to take responsibility for mistakes.

People do not like an aggressive approach.

People are reluctant to commit to something without their managers' approval.

An assertive nature is seen as self-centered, and impolite words are not appreciated.

Smile at all times, even when you are angry.

People should keep calm and be polite at all times.

People will change jobs readily if they are not happy.

People may not speak out to managers about their dissatisfaction, but they may resign.

### Attitude towards changes

People are fearful of trying new things.

People may resist change and be stubborn.

People may change their behavior to protect themselves if they do not understand the issue in question.

People sometimes do not answer the phone or email if they are not happy with something.

People consider challenges as threats.

Changes can be viewed as challenging and improvements equal to more work.

### Management

It is necessary to give a clear explanation of how to get things done. It is best to give detailed guidance.

There are sensitive issues that should not be discussed, such as religious or political matters.

Micromanagement is common.

When a task is delegated, it is safer to monitor it, even if you are dealing with managers.

People are afraid of addressing issues with their bosses. Instead, they gossip (discuss) together.

There is a family working style.

Decision-making is not delegated.

Power distance is crucial in getting things done. Only business owners and very top management have decision power.

## The reality of local workforce capability

The capacity of the local workforce is lower than among those you might have met before at workshops.

The English levels of the workforce are limited.

Analytical skills are limited.

It can take till the last minute to organize things.

People find it difficult to fully express themselves and to be fully understood.

People may find it difficult to communicate what they want.

People are not good at multi-tasking.

People lack attention to details.

People are not too ambitious.

People are afraid to try to "think outside the box".

Initiatives by locals are few.

## 4.4 COMPARATIVE THOUGHTS OF EXPATS AND LOCALS

Men come from Mars and Women come from Venus - A summary of how expats and locals think differently:

|   | Locals' thoughts about expats | Expats' thoughts about locals |
|---|-------------------------------|-------------------------------|
| 1 | Too pushy | Too slow |
| 2 | Too aggressive | Too shy |
| 3 | Talk too much | Not outspoken |
| 4 | Arrogant | Too humble |
| 5 | Cold, distant | Too emotional |
| 6 | Not kind, caring | Not professional, bring personal issues to work |

| 7 | Too blunt, shouting, rude | Hide their real thoughts and emotions |
|---|---|---|
| 8 | Don't listen and don't understand Myanmar | I have lots of experience and qualifications |
| 9 | I cannot say "No" to others directly | They say "Yes" but do not deliver their promises |
| 10 | Strict, on time | Do not respect schedules and deadlines |
| 11 | Greedy, only results-oriented, selfish | Not ambitious |
| 12 | Their thinking is too complex | They lack analytical skills |
| 13 | Don't respect elder colleagues | Why respect without any proper reason |
| 14 | Too demanding | Have to upgrade local skills effectively |
| 15 | Have many strange ideas | Do not think outside the box |

# CHAPTER 5

# TO SUCCEED IN THE WORKPLACE – COMMUNICATING WHEN YES IS NO

## 5.1 HOW TO DEAL WITH "WHEN YES IS NO"

As mentioned before, many expats say they wish they had known before coming to Myanmar that "Yes" does not necessarily mean "Yes" here. Let's look at the ramifications of this aspect of Myanmar culture more closely.

The following story would not be an unusual case for a new expat to encounter in Myanmar.

An expat gives an assignment to a local colleague and receives the answer "Yes, I will do it," in a prompt manner. Then when the deadline clocks in, the expat is stunned to discover that things have not been done yet! Or it may happen that things are done, but the results are not at all what he expected.

What happened?

I recall a story of an ASEAN expat when she first came here to work.

### THE GOOGLE SEARCH ASSIGNMENT

*The expat gave the two female colleagues the research assignment to find out which universities offer human resources as a subject in their curriculum and the related faculty contacts. The two young ladies, one with excellent English skills, said, "Yes, yes, yes," nodding their heads continuously. They seemed very enthusiastic and confident, and they repeated "Yes," when the expat asked, "Are you sure you can do it in a week?"*

*The ASEAN expat felt so glad that she had dynamic colleagues with a "can do" attitude.*

*Then, after seven days, she was astonished that she had heard nothing from them. She had to actively seek them out for an update about their progress. The simple reply she got from them was: "We are too busy with other tasks." Trying to repress her surprise, the expat attempted to find out the obstacles by asking different questions relating to all their other tasks.*

*It turned out that other tasks had not impeded their progress on the project. The two female colleagues had not done the assignment because they were not sure how to find potential universities or how to check if a university offered the HR subject because they did not know how to obtain the phone numbers.*

*When she gave the assignment, the expat had said, "Please 'Google' for universities' names." However, they were not used to using Google for information searching!*

"Why did not they ask me about it? It is just so easy to ask and do the right things than to keep quiet and fail the assignment!" The expat expressed her frustration.

### THE COOKED EGGS AT THE MODERN RESTAURANT

*An expat went to a restaurant that usually catered to office staff of a local office building. The waiter and waitress were well-dressed and appeared very polished and polite.*

*With his Burmese skills, the expat ordered two eggs well cooked on both sides, which is different from the typical local style of leaving the yolk uncooked.*

*When he got the food, the expat was disappointed that it was not what he wanted but was exactly the same as any fried eggs done in the regular local style.*

*He asked a local manager (his colleague) with good English skills to help him, and she confirmed his desire clearly. He was confident that he would get what he wanted with her intervention.*

*Again, the eggs were brought to him with the yolk uncooked.*

The expat was sure that the local manager conveyed his message properly to the waiter. The local manager later shared that the waiter did not ask any questions about the particular order from her, even though it was different from the usual style. Then the waiter may give the wrong instruction to the chef. Or if he gave the right instruction, the chef might not ask any questions about the particularly unusual order, and assumed that he understood the waiter well enough.

## "ASKING BACK" IS OUT OF THE ORDINARY

This leads to a corollary about the Myanmar culture. Very few people ask for clarification.

So "Yes" may mean "No." In fact, answering "Yes" to a given task might simply mean "Yes, I heard you." It does not mean the task was properly understood. A "Yes" answer might really mean "I'm not sure if it will be done, " or "I'm not sure it will be done properly."

In Myanmar, many expats say "*People here are too shy to ask questions for clarification when they do not understand what was said*," or "*People saying yes or nodding does not mean that they will actually carry out the tasks.*"

Misunderstanding in communication can be found anywhere in the world. Yet in Myanmar, it is a common issue between expats and local colleagues, especially when the expats are newcomers to Myanmar.

People often say "Yes," because they are hesitant to say "No" here. If you ask, "Do you like this option?" instead of saying "No," they may answer "I am still thinking," or "Maybe," or "I am not sure."

Sometimes people say, "Yes, I will come to the meeting" and then they do not show up.

Expats think: *"People say they will do something, but then they do not do it."* On the other hand, local people think *they are trying not to offend expats by agreeing to do something rather than saying "No."*

Survival Rule 2, "Anadeh" (incl. "Saving Face") is why such things happen. Communication is indirect here. As mentioned in Chapter 1, "Anadeh" is the consideration of others - not wanting to hurt others' feelings or not wanting to offend or embarrass or disappoint others, which includes Saving Face. Saying "No" to someone's face seems disappointing to a Myanmar - he or she will feel bad refusing or refuting a supervisor's or senior's wishes.

Many local HR and other professionals emphasize that expats should take note that local people typically do not "ask back" (ask clarifying questions) even when they do not understand something. A local professional with over ten years' experience working with expats comments that in the above case, "The ladies did not ask back because they did not want to appear incompetent. They thought that they would try to figure out what to do later." They are applying the "Saving Face" rule so as not to embarrass themselves or others.

Plus, due to the practice of Hierarchy - the Respect of Seniors and Elders, local colleagues do not "ask back" when told something by expats (who often are their managers) even if they do not have a full understanding of what was said. Doing so would be considered a challenge to a senior or an elder's authority, which would be rude.

## *How to know when "Yes is Yes"?*

How, then, does an expat know when local colleagues really mean "Yes"? Check back, please, to make sure you are properly understood.

A local HR Director who has 28 years of working with foreigners (both overseas and in Myanmar) says "*Local people tend to assume things when they are not very clear.*" Then you should "ask back" to see how they understand the matter and ask for details as to how they plan to accomplish the task. For example: "How do you plan to do this?" will help reveal areas where the steps to accomplishing a task are not understood.

If you want to know their real opinion about something, bringing them two options and ask them to choose one. For example, say, "Between option 1 and option 2, which do you think is better?"

Understanding should be confirmed by going into very specific details. Short answers may be very misleading.

**Summary**

|  | Locals | Expats |
|---|---|---|
|  | Say "Yes." Do not want to offend expats by asking questions even when they do not really understand. Think that they will figure it out later. | Think that locals understand and will do it on time. |
|  | May not do it. | Think that "Locals do not deliver on their promises." |

| Solutions | Expats "ask back" different questions to see how far and how well locals understand what is said, e.g., "How will you do this?" Or "Which option do you choose between 1 and 2?" |
|---|---|
| Solutions (long-term) | Expats shares with locals: "Please 'ask back' to understand things in detail." Give examples of negative consequences if there is no proper understanding of the tasks. Provide Business English Communications training. |

## 5.2 HOW TO USE SIMPLE LANGUAGE TO MAKE IT WORK

Language is a recurrent barrier for expats working abroad. It is not atypical for those working in Myanmar.

A local friend of mine who works for the commercial department of a Western organization shared that he was confused reading emails from his American superior.

*The emails were sent to local business partners. After reading those emails, he was not sure if the American expat's answer as to whether they could import certain products to Myanmar was "Yes" or "No." This was in spite of the fact that he had good English skills.*

*His superior is also a diplomatic person; he used subtle and sophisticated language more suited to interacting with other native speakers. For example, instead of saying, "I do not think so," he would say, "May I beg to differ with you?"*

That caused a lot of misunderstanding between him and his local business partners. Thus, the potential co-operation between them was slower in progress than it would have been otherwise.

Another grammar form that confuses locals is the negative form, which usually is used to soften the language.

A European expat shared that when he first came here, he cast questions in the negative several times and the results were the same – confusion.

*He asked a local colleague in a procurement function: "Don't you want to ask them for more details of their drafted sales proposal?" and got the reply, "No, I want to ask them."*

*At first, he was a bit confused to receive an answer with a negative and a positive as a reply. Then he asked, "Do you want to ask them?" and the answer was, "Yes, I want to ask them."*

*Another time when he asked another local colleague: "Won't you come to the inauguration of our client?" he got the reply "Yes."*

*Suspecting that she was trying to say she wouldn't come, he asked again: "Will you come there?" and she said, "No, I will not come there."*

Expats should not ask questions in negative forms, such as: "Don't you…" or "Aren't you….?" It complicates the locals' understanding! You will get back confusing answers. You may have to ask further questions to get a clear answer.

Many expats discover that the English skills of local

colleagues are less than what they envisioned. As mentioned in Chapter 3, generally speaking, the English skills of most of the local workforce are modest due to the limited capacity of the education system and their lack of international exposure.

An expat coming from Holland confirmed that he needs to be very simple in communicating with local colleagues for better efficiency in communication. For example, if he wants a person to report him by email the progress of a given task, he says "Please email me every day about its progress."

The old saying *"Less is more"* holds true in Myanmar!

**Summary**

|  | Locals | Expats |
|---|---|---|
|  | Are confused | Use subtle English language devices |
|  | Answer unclearly | Use negative-form questions |
| Solutions | Expats use simple language. Expats do not use negative-form questions. Provide Business English Communications training. | |

## 5.3 HOW TO GET THE BEST HELP FROM AN INTERPRETER

*The newly arrived general manager of a modernizing gym center found it hard to communicate with his local colleagues. Only a few of them had good English skills.*

*After trying to explain to local colleagues about the new kinds of machines they should import for the gym center, he could see that they did not comprehend. He decided to try an interpreter. A local colleague translated for him to over twenty others.*

*When the interpreter translated the explanation about the useful functions of the new, modern machines, he mentioned the machines of another very famous gym center. Every local trainer knew about its high tech machines.*

*His colleagues now understood clearly what needed to be done.*

Again, language is often an obstacle for an expat in working with local colleagues. Even in a multinational working environment, language barriers still cause numerous communication issues. Not everyone can comprehend English well. Expats working in local companies are the most subject to such communication glitches.

Under those circumstances, acquiring an interpreter is not a bad idea. There are several reasons for doing so. First, the interpreter helps expats communicate their messages in the Myanmar language so everyone can understand. Second, when locals do not understand the message well, they are more comfortable to "ask back" a local interpreter than to "ask back" an expat about it, as mentioned in the previous section. For both these reasons, a Burmese interpreter is a desirable option. Furthermore, a Burmese interpreter knows local examples and how to help colleagues understand most efficiently.

*An Asian expat managing a logistics service branch of over twenty local colleagues shared that instead of recruiting employees who all have good English skills, she focuses on recruiting managers/team leaders with good English. These managers help communicate her messages to the rest of local colleagues.*

*For example, an accountant may not need to have very good English skills, but the chief accountant needs them.*

*Doing things this way saves her company lots of time and money.*

In the various contexts of corporate meetings, events, and training, interpreters are needed.

### Summary

A local interpreter will help with the following:

- Translate expats' messages to other local colleagues.
- Answer their questions further in various ways that they understand.
- Serve as a bridge for explaining cultural differences and clearing up misunderstandings on both sides (if capable).

## 5.4 HOW TO UTILIZE THE POWER OF POSITIVE LANGUAGE

The truth is, positive language works everywhere in the world! The power of positive language is even more significant in Myanmar.

## "A GOOD MOUTH RULES THE COUNTRY" (MYANMAR PROVERB)

Most of Myanmar local colleagues want to learn new skills and knowledge to improve their performance; however, many expats find that criticism is not a good way to help them realize their shortcomings and make improvements.

If they criticize local colleagues, the outcomes are the reverse of what they hope for. Again, communication requires gentle, indirect subtlety. Direct criticism would be considered "rude"; it would fall into the violation of Survival Rule 2 - "Anadeh" ("Saving Face" included).

### CRITICISM IS DETRIMENTAL

*Kind words can warm for three winters, while harsh words can chill even in the heat of summer.* (Chinese proverb)

A story comes from an ASEAN expat who has been in Myanmar for a year.

*The expat is hard working and has a broad local network and regional connections for his company's business of distributing spare parts.*

*He is eager to develop his company's business in Myanmar quickly and tries to coach his sales employees every day. He is continually concerned with how to make a strategy, a plan, how to approach industrial clients more aggressively, and how to meet them and build up relationships.*

*He pushes his sales employees every day. When they did not meet the sales target, he felt like they did not follow all his coaching. If they had, they would be much more efficient than the salespeople of key competitors.*

*Disappointed, he shouted at them: "Why did not you try? It is so easy to get more new clients!" He added, "You need to follow all my training strictly." He then demanded, "Everyday report to me in detail what you do and what you plan for the next day."*

*He still needs to recruit new sales employees every three to six months.*

*His subordinates often resign under the pressure he places them under. Some have left, even though the salaries they get at the new place of employment are lower than the salaries under him.*

Sadly, there have been cases of an expat shouting at local colleagues with the consequence that the local colleagues resigned not long afterward.

As mentioned in Chapter 1: "**Shouting is unacceptable**" for locals. It violates the survival rules of Anadeh (incl. Saving Face). Further, with the insecure self that was mentioned in Chapter 2, due to Myanmar's traumatic history, it is not easy for locals to stand up to pressure and criticism. Also, in Myanmar "Resistance to Change" is a strong defense mechanism due mostly to the traumatic history embedded in their mindset.

An American expat shared that after four years of working

in Myanmar, she learned: *"Do not mention it when someone makes a mistake; do not correct people; do not argue."*

It is much worse if you criticize a local senior (Survival Rule 1 – Hierarchy).

*Another General Manager (GM) coming from an Asian country is in business development for one business branch of a leading business group here.*

*"He is weird," his local colleagues said of him. They considered him arrogant and not very co-operative with other departments. For example, when they asked him for supporting documentation for his business trip invoices, he ignored them.*

*"He always criticizes us," they say. He is the one in Chapter 4, "A Story about Mr. Singapore." Whatever happens, he always says, "People in Singapore are not like that", "People's skills here are too low (as compared to people in Singapore)", and "I need to hire more expats to work effectively", etc.*

*Things accumulated for over a year, and it got to the point that the Asian expat, with all his many years of experience in developing businesses in Singapore, did not even hesitate to criticize the group CEO (a local) in front of others. He addressed the CEO's limitation in business strategy and the fact that he did not carry out his promise to hire more expats, etc.*

*After such a public dressing down, the local CEO later said to his local colleagues, "If he does not resign, I will."*

The result, as you may know already from a previous chapter, is that the expat had to resign. He had not expected that.

### POSITIVE LANGUAGE WORKS

It is part of human nature that, under normal circumstances, people do not want to be forced to do things. The better way is to inspire them. Thus, giving local colleagues compliments when they do things right is necessary.

A financial analyst for a reputable, international energy company, who had over seven years' experience working with expats, said that when working with local colleagues, expats should *"encourage them, and appreciate them for their good or even okay performances. You will see how much better that works."*

She spoke very positively about her Spanish manager: *"We all love to work with her as she does not ignore our conversations, our thoughts, and our wishes. She cares for us and encourages us very well."*

Encouragement is a good way for people to take small risks, especially when things are new to them, beyond their experience, education or imagination. When one makes a mistake, it is better to coach the person for improvement's sake than to criticize him or her.

A chief representative of a financial service company shares an experience of how he behaved when a local colleague under his management made a mistake. He has lived in Myanmar for six years.

*"The first thing I do is not scold her, because that would make it worse.*

*The second thing I do is to sit down with her and explain so that she can fully understand the consequences of the mistake and how to prevent it from happening again next time."*

*This colleague forgot to check the bank balance and the financial obligations that the office needed to pay to the government tax office in addition to the office rental fees. The result was that all the required payments were due at the same time, and the balance was not enough to cover it. It would take two months to liaise with the mother company to get the money.*

*The chief representative then used his own money to pay the amounts while waiting for the money to come from the mother company.*

*Still, the colleague has worked with him ever since the office opened. Happily, he finds her making professional progress.*

Coaching a person when he or she makes a mistake should only be done in a private meeting.

Again, "Saving Face" is critical in the Golden Land.

## Summary

|  | Expats | Local |
|---|---|---|
|  | Criticize (even professionally) local colleagues' mistakes. | Feel embarrassed, "Lose Face". Possibly are not able to change behaviors. |
| Solutions | Expats do not criticize local colleagues' mistakes. Calmly explain all the consequences of the errors and how to prevent it from happening again in the future. | |
| Solutions (long-term) | Expats give compliments, encourage local colleagues whenever possible. Provide necessary training - Critical Thinking and Problem Solving Course. | |

# CHAPTER 6

# TO SUCCEED IN THE WORKPLACE – RELATIONSHIPS ARE KEY

## 6.1 HOW TO AVOID "OUT OF SIGHT, OUT OF MIND"

The above proverb is testified to in Myanmar. It holds true for many people in business and organizations.

*"EMAILS DO NOT WORK HERE. ONLY FACE-TO-FACE DOES!"*

This is the assessment of an American expat coming from New York after working in Myanmar for six years. She has been in both capacities, as a manager in an international NGO, and as an independent consultant for many government officers.

*She recollected her memorable experience of writing many letters to different local people and organizations, i.e., sending a letter to a service provider about their services, or inquiring about meeting them, only to be met with silence. Sometimes she sent letters to the bookshop owners who were buying books from the NGO, asking about the sales status of the books. Again, she was met with silence.*

*The information she sought was necessary and nothing top secret. It could be supposed that the people providing the information would feel at ease responding her, or informing her that they did not have the information.*

*She then re-sent her letters several times in case the recipients were very busy and had missed her emails. But the results were the same: no replies.*

*The reality, when she found out about it, was not what she expected.*

*She only became efficient at contacting people and getting information and meetings when she picked up her phone to get their responses or to call them to arrange face-to-face meetings.*

*That worked very well.*

## ATTAINING FURTHER INFORMATION AND BUILDING THE RELATIONSHIP

A face-to-face meeting provides much more information, avoids misunderstanding due to the language barrier, and provide "hints" for communication. As mentioned, Myanmar people do not, as a rule, communicate openly or directly.

Many business concepts, methods, techniques are still very new here; thus, detailed explanations are usually needed.

There are still many things that are still considered to be "sensitive". Local people do not want to put such things in black-and-white emails. For example, laws and regulations are complicated - some details need to be explained further verbally. Law could have variations in interpretations and applications depending on the government offices or courts involved.

Moreover, in-person encounters help to clarify things. If an expat sees that someone is hesitant to do something, the expat can ask the reason why, or at least ask leading questions to ferret out the reason. Such things cannot be done via emails.

In the end, it takes time and effort to build up good relationships. In person meetings will undoubtedly be an integral part of it. Relationships and trust are crucial to doing business in Asia, and particularly in Myanmar. In a state where the "rule of law" is still weak, trust has to be gained before doing business activities. Relating to this, many Western expats are surprised to find out the extent of a relationship prerequisite for a business deal.

Continuous face-to-face meetings are always the best way when seeking possible cooperation with a potential business partner. Several initial meetings are not enough to establish "trust" for subsequent communication in emails, common as they may be in the international business world. Without face-to-face meetings, mutual understanding, trust, and subsequently good relationships cannot be established in Myanmar.

## THE FRESH USAGE OF THE INTERNET

Myriad expats experienced "out of sight, out of mind" stories in varied communication contexts in Myanmar. Sometimes, the reason is simple – many local people do not use email often or do not use it at all. Sometimes the reason is more complex.

Just a few years ago, even using a mobile phone was rare in Myanmar, let alone utilizing the internet and emails. Sim cards and calling rates were very costly prior to the recent establishment of foreign telecom operators such as Telenor, Ooredoo, and Mytel.

Even for the majority of local people who access the internet using Facebook and Viber very frequently, utilizing emails for business is still not common. It happens more in local and small businesses. People would prefer using Facebook than email even in business – i.e, for sending office documents. Facebook is extremely popular in Myanmar. As noted previously, people search for things on Facebook instead of using Google.

The benefits of using email are increasingly apparent in Myanmar, though. You can get email responses very quickly from local partners or employees. A friend of mine in the service sector said that she would send invoices by email all the time to international clients without the need to send the printout.

When I was researching this book, I used email and got

responses from local professionals via email. Notably, the ones I deal with have good English skills and are quite used to working in international organizations.

For international and many local large companies alike, email is an active communication channel.

### WHEN TO HAVE FACE-TO-FACE MEETINGS?

Face-to-face meetings are always appropriate to meet up with potential local partners.

In organizations, many local professionals recommend that expats have face-to-face meetings with their direct reports regularly. This is critical to understanding the progress of their assignments and to monitoring the results. Moreover, it helps to minimize the "avoidance of reporting bad news and confrontation" – a common cultural conflict that expats encounter in Myanmar.

Giving guidance for the deployment of a new product or organizing a skill training session should not be done via email. This is to make sure things are properly understood. When coaching a local colleague after he or she makes a mistake, a face-to-face meeting is, of course, the best way.

When communicating with government officers, face-to-face meetings are expected. For example, companies may want to meet with general ministry directors to enquire about the market situation, policies for foreign businesses in certain sectors, or procedures for opening a new ministry-related business, etc. face-to-face meetings are a good way to learn more about how the system works and are a way to show respect to the authority.

### THE SUCCESS OF A MULTI-FACETED CONNECTION

Here is a unique story about how an expat made a partnership with a famous tycoon.

*The Australian expat (originally ASEAN) employed a very intense and unique approach. Instead of befriending the tycoon (the business owner) who was much older than he was, he befriended the tycoon's two sons, who were younger and nearer his age.*

*He then accompanied them to all possible occasions: gatherings with friends, Buddhist festivals, on their travels, etc. He went everywhere with them - to their offices, home, restaurants, bars, golf courses, overseas, etc. His wife often saw him coming back home very late, i.e., 1 a.m. or 3 a.m. He was sometimes drunk after a night of hanging out with those affluent guys.*

*As an expat with abundant international experience, he served as an informal consultant to them about how to do business internationally and more professionally. The young guys liked this very much.*

*In return, he got to know all about their habits, hobbies, and personalities. He knew what they liked to wear, to eat, to drink, and how they liked to play. Soon he knew everyone they knew and all their connections. From them he came to understand the real power structure in Myanmar and how it worked.*

*He was friends with them for over three years. The more time he spent with them and the more he pleased them in various ways, the closer they became. Through them, he got leads to lots of elite connections in Myanmar, both in business and in government.*

*He eventually landed some significant business projects, in which he played a vital part, through the connections they led him to.*

**Summary**

|  | Expats | Locals (potential partners, partners, colleagues) |
|---|---|---|
|  | Email to discuss business matters. | May not reply, or may not reply in detail. |
|  | Feel strange. | Feel uncomfortable replying through email (it is time-consuming, it does not convey enough meaning). Sensitive matters are not to be written in emails. |
| Solutions | Phone to arrange face-to-face meetings. | |
| Solutions (long-term) | Use both – face-to-face meetings for important matters and emails for non-essential ones. (Depends on the others' habit of using emails). Establish multifaceted connections. | |

## 6.2 HOW TO BE SOFT, POLITE, AND SMILING (NOT AGGRESSIVE)

Myanmar people habitually communicate softly and politely. During six years of living here, I rarely encountered anyone speaking in a loud voice to another person.

As mentioned in Chapter 1, gentle indirect subtlety is expected.

### *A WISE MAN NEVER REVEALS HIS ANGER (MYANMAR PROVERB)*

Article 1.4 in Chapter 1 provides an illustration of how shouting is unacceptable in Myanmar. If an expat shows annoyance or strong negative emotions, local colleagues do not respond positively. They are very sensitive when it comes to that.

Repressing anger or other emotions, however, could be strange for many foreigners who are used to showing their feelings more openly. It is worth doing, though. A Western lawyer shares that after working in Myanmar for three years, he discovered the most important thing for him is "*to focus on being polite and calm all the time.*"

*Whenever I raise my voice, or lose my temper, my local colleagues seem to be sensitive and fearful of me. If I a shout a bit about something, even if I am not shouting at my local colleagues (i.e., I am shouting about the strange behavior of a client, or a new policy of the government), they are also uncomfortable and avoid contact with me.*

*If there is an urgent matter happening at such a time, they do not dare to report it to me. They are hesitant to talk with a person who is not in a good mood.*

*They are frightened.*

## ASSERTIVENESS AND AGGRESSIVENESS VS. SOFT, POLITE AND SMILING

As an effect of Survival Rule 2 – Anadeh, asserting one's view in a direct and dogmatic manner is not considered positive here.

Many local professionals disclose that local colleagues usually think expats are too "aggressive" to get the job done. "Very pushing!" they say.

An HR Manager from a major business group shares a story about her expat manager:

*My HR general manager from an ASEAN country is a very dynamic and smart guy.*

*He has a good relationship with the chairman. The chairman expects him to re-structure their HR function to serve the group business properly.*

*To do it, one of the things he insists his local subordinates achieve is an accurate salary survey for the various vacancies in the group business areas, such as banking, energy, telecom, real estate, hotels, etc.*

*The problem is that in Myanmar there is no accurate data on these positions. Moreover, the salary range for each role fluctuates a lot as the market is still new and is not mature yet.*

*Further, he wants to achieve international standard performance appraisals for all business functions in two years. This thing is also hard to achieve given the complex current situation of the group, as well as the country's economic situation, and the lack of skills and data.*

*He, however, insists strongly on doing all this to get the desired results. He pushes us too much, every two days, about carrying out his plan in an effective manner. Sometimes he loses his temper. Indeed, many things are new to us, and also we cannot supply him with what he requires in time.*

*It creates a tense atmosphere in our HR function, and many people are upset.*

*Currently, 8 out of 12 people in the department have resigned.*

It is not easy to keep calm all the time in Myanmar, many expats say.

There is much pressure on expats during their contract terms of normally two or three years. The companies that hired them expect very positive business results, while on the ground there are too many challenges. There are infrastructure issues such as limited internet speed, electricity cuts, congested traffic in Yangon, and the lack of skills in the workforce. Then there are superstructure issues such as changing laws, the new government's operation, etc.

From the local colleagues' perspective, the business targets assigned to them by expats are too high and the deadlines are too short. There are many hindrances in the way of realizing the objectives. Local colleagues sometimes think expats do not glean the situation in Myanmar very well and thus set unrealistic business goals.

Assertiveness, which sometimes turns into aggressiveness, distresses local colleagues. It makes things worse. This is due, as mentioned in Chapter 2, to the traumatic history of Myanmar. The people are already fearful inside. Plus, they are used to behaving in a gentle manner.

Being a bit softer is a much better approach. It is in harmony with the Myanmar people, who are generally emotional and heart-driven.

Politeness is expected here. As mentioned before, another HR director for an international company with over ten years' experience working with expats shares: *"Local colleagues very much hate it when an expat uses strong words such as 'f\*ck' or 'sh\*t'."* They feel it is disrespectful.

Instead of being aggressive, an expat should offer local colleagues smiles! It is the universal language. *"A smile goes a long way in Myanmar,"* the above HR Director advises. *"Local people see your smile and feel that you are very friendly and approachable. They then feel comfortable connecting with you."*

Similarly, an American expat says she learns that a person "*should smile all the time in Myanmar, even if one is angry.*"

Please note that locals can smile when they have made mistakes. There is a Myanmar proverb "*A child cries when he feels ashamed while an adult tries to laugh when he feels so.*" They take their mistakes seriously; that is why they smile.

Smile, please!

### Summary

|  | Expats | Locals |
|---|---|---|
|  | Sometimes are hot-tempered or show strong negative emotions. | Feel scared, stressed. Are not able to work well. |
|  | Use strong slang words such as f*ck, sh*t (even when not directly to colleagues). | Feel not comfortable, disrespected. Dislike it. |
| Solutions | Soften things; do things in a polite and gentle manner. | |
| Solutions (long-term) | Keep calm. Smile. Share with locals that in other countries, a show of anger is usual in working contexts. (Illustrate by video, movies, etc.) | |

## 6.3 HOW TO SHOW YOUR CARE AND KINDNESS

*KINDNESS IS THE LANGUAGE OF THE SOUL*

*(ANONYMOUS PROVERB)*

The corporate environment in Myanmar is often a place where "The Heart Wins the Mind", as mentioned in Chapter 3. People here are more emotional than rational. The feminine culture focuses more on building good relationships and maintaining a friendly atmosphere than on pure results-orientation and competitiveness.

Local colleagues are motivated when they feel they are cared for. Simply put, this means their managers show kindness to them. "**Kindness**" (kyin-na-hmu) is a very common notion and a requirement here.

An HR manager of a joint venture demonstrates the differences of a too rational expat and a caring expat:

*If a subordinate comes late for work, there are two possible scenarios of behaviour for expats.*

*In scenario 1, an expat would say: "I see you are late every day. It is awful. Can you make sure you never do it again? Okay?"*

*In scenario 2, rather than that, an expat would ask: "Why are you late every day? What are your difficulties?"*

*The staff member may say something like: "I need to bring my kids to the new school and it is farther away than the old school. It is tough for me to be on time."*

*Then the expat says: "Can you possibly wake up earlier? Then you can bring them to school earlier, before coming to work. Do you think that might work better? Unfortunately, if you continue to be late, your annual bonus will be deducted because it is linked to your performance appraisal and so is a salary bonus."*

*The staff member might then say: "Yes, I will try that. Thank you very much."*

The expat in scenario 1 would be seen as being too cold and uncaring toward his subordinates. His only desire is for the staff to be on time to get results. He just gives orders, rules, and regulations! He is very autocratic and distant.

The expat in scenario 2 would come across as caring, because he tries to understand the difficulties of his staff member and helps him to solve his problems.

Another HR Manager of a local business group shares about her favourite expats among the thirty she has known in the last four years.

*He is a European Chief Financial Officer of the group.*

*From the first, he tried to learn about Burmese culture and some of the Burmese language. He is very caring and kind to his subordinates. He is close and friendly as well. Sometimes he brings them to famous hotel restaurants for international buffets so they can enjoy more fun in life and they can build relationships with one another there.*

*He asks about people's situations, their job difficulties, their family situations, hobbies, etc. Sometimes he goes with them to local festivals in Thingyan or to Thadingyut festivals. In the new year, he gives lucky money to all ten people in his department. When he comes back from Europe, he brings chocolates or gifts for them. Sometimes his wife cooks things for him to deliver there for them. He even helps people carry heavy files without hesitation.*

*At first, people opposed him when he wanted to apply the ERP system to the group finance system. They were afraid they would lose their jobs due to their lack of technology and other necessary skills.*

*But he tried to explain why the company needed it and trained them in how to apply the system effectively. Plus, all his care and kindness make his team love him very much. They spread his good nature to other employees in the company. After about six months, things are okay for him in deploying his mission.*

*Now he has been in Myanmar for over three years.*

### Summary

|  | Expats | Locals |
|---|---|---|
|  | Only give orders and want results. | Feel expats are not caring, not kind. |
|  | No interest in personal matters of locals. Don't mingle with locals. | Feel expats too cold, distant. Afraid to approach them when needed. |

| Solutions | Be interested in fundamental personal matters of local colleagues such as age, education, ethnicity, family, house location, etc. Regular meetings out of the office to build relationships. |
|---|---|
| Solutions (long-term) | Mingle with locals in local contexts. Chances to mingle – meetings, meals, monthly festivals, personal events (birthdays, weddings, family members' funerals). |

## 6.4 HOW TO PAY RESPECT WHICH HOLDS EVERYTHING

Many local employees think that many expats do not respect them. Lack of respect manifests in various ways.

When I asked more than fifty local HR heads and professionals: *"What should an expat do to work more effectively in Myanmar?"*, the answer is repeated again and again: "**Respect the locals.**"

In keeping with Survival Rule 1 - Hierarchy works, the Myanmar people have a tradition of respecting senior and older people. Most of Myanmar employees thus hold respect for expats, who are usually their supervisors or managers.

At the same time, they expect respect in return. They hope expats will respect their religion, their culture, and themselves.

Respect means respecting the Buddha, not pointing at anything with feet, not touching anyone's head, and not using strong slang. Respect means not shouting or yelling at people. Respect means Saving Face.

Respect means knowing Hierarchy, Anadeh, and gentle, indirect subtlety.

Mutual respect is a foundation to build up mutual understanding, acceptance, and ultimately trust.

### EMPATHY AND RESPECT

To be concise, what is "respect"? According to a reputable online dictionary, it is "To value or regard the worth of people and things and to treat them with consideration, care, and concern."

Ko Maung, a repat with over ten years working in the ASEAN region, comments, *"Please understand that Myanmar was in a dark age for many decades and it strongly affected all people. Even if they seem to lack experience or skills, please do not look down on them, and do not make harsh comments."*

The story below happened in one European garment factory in an industrial zone.

*The Asian expat is a tough one, and he is very strict in his job of quality control. He often makes harsh comments to ensure the quality of the garment products. For just a small mistake he spots in a shirt, for example, he will throw it down to the "error area" and shout angrily to local workers nearby. They are not happy about it.*

*One day, there was a meeting in an office room. The Asian expat's hand slipped, and he dropped a water bottle that touched a local supervisor. The local supervisor felt insulted and screamed emotionally.*

*Many other local workers heard that and ran into the room. As they mobbed the room, the local workers turned their anger on the QC expat and told him that he was too arrogant and insulting. They demanded that he go back home (a neighbor country).*

*Was this an excellent chance they took to return all the harshness they were given by him before?*

*When it was reported to the Township Labour office, they asked a company representative to come to meet them. They went to the factory to inspect the case. The expat is to apologize to the local supervisor in public.*

*Most critically, he has to write a letter guaranteeing not to repeat any of his inappropriate actions. If he does so, he will be sent back home immediately.*

For local colleagues, it is, of course, not a good thing to feel looked down upon or to be thought of as not smart or irresponsible. It is impractical to expect Myanmar employees to have the same skills and experience as those in other neighboring ASEAN countries. It is the result of the dark history of their country, not their faults.

Life is still very tough for the majority of local people, given that Myanmar is still one of the poorest countries on the globe. The lives of people are constrained due to the limited infrastructure – education and health care, the low average income, traffic issues, electricity issues, etc. Yet people are mostly honest, helpful, generous, and have their dignity.

Ultimately, without the contribution of local colleagues, an expat cannot be successful working here.

## MR. NO NO NO AND RESPECT

Some expats come to Myanmar in "consulting roles" and they come up with their judgments about everything quickly.

They pretend to know everything here. They then assert that many things are not proper here. They use the words "No, No, No" often to show their opinion about inappropriate things in Myanmar. Thus, they maintain that things need to be changed as per their advice.

Local people, in reality, think they know nothing about Myanmar. Their quick judgment does not closely adhere to the particular domestic situation.

People want change for good, but if a consultant does not "touch the ground," how can good advice be obtained?

They would think Mr. No No No is arrogant and disrespectful.

Respect also goes with being humble. In the West, the great ancient philosopher Aristotle said: "*The only thing I know is I know nothing.*" In the East, Lao Tzu says: "*Knowing thyself is the beginning of wisdom.*"

If a thing has been done for years, there are reasons for doing it that way. "*To write a 'Wikipedia' without knowing a* '*w*'" is a Myanmar saying that refers to an arrogant person who knows nothing but acts as if he knows everything.

Comprehending a "w" prior to writing a Wikipedia is, indeed, a must!

**Summary**

|  | Expats | Locals |
|---|---|---|
|  | Act in disrespectful manners. Give harsh comments or criticize rudely. | Feel expats are disrespectful. Strongly dislike. |
|  | Pretend to know everything here. Assume only their ways are proper. | Feel expats are arrogant and do not understand Myanmar reality. |
| Solutions | Apply all the "Dos and Don'ts," Survival Rules 1, 2, and gentle, indirect subtlety. Apologize sincerely for forgetting the rules and offending locals. | |
| Solutions (long-term) | Spend time on the ground and learn more about Myanmar's situation. Spend time comprehending the reality before giving advice. | |

# CHAPTER 7

# TO SUCCEED IN THE WORKPLACE – MICROMANAGEMENT, RECRUITMENT, AND TRAINING

## 7.1 HOW TO MICROMANAGE

Every place on earth has its customs for doing things in a certain way. The example in Chapter 5, "When Yes is No", shows the need to micromanage in Myanmar.

Let's refer back to an earlier story:

*An ASEAN expat gave two female colleagues the research assignment to find out information about what universities offer the subject of human resources in their curriculum. They were not used to using Google for information searching, but they did not let her know that until she found out they had not done the assignment they had promised to do.*

*The issue was only resolved when the ASEAN expat gave them very detailed instructions on how to do it, using the 5W & 1H method: explaining what-which, who, whom, when, where and how.*

*The expat needed to follow the progress of things very*

*carefully. When there was an issue, she needed to help them resolve it on the spot.*

As mentioned in Chapter 3, local colleagues are unfamiliar with many international standards. Most of the local workforce lacks international exposure. The international standards that expats expect of them are often well beyond their experience, education, and imaginations. That is why detailed instructions and coaching are needed.

The truth is, many expats in Myanmar find themselves operating in "micromanagement" style, which they had not expected. They have to furnish their subordinates (reports) with detailed instructions, coach them, and monitor the process even though the task has been delegated. In a way, they relinquish what they call "professional management" and adopt "micromanagement."

An expat from Europe who has lived here over four years puts it: "*People seem to pay little attention to details.*"

*He gave the example of the banner design and printout for his beverage promotion program. When he checked things at the last, he usually found that he had to ask for the color in the layout or printout to be changed, or he would sometimes find a small error in the printout material, and it had to be changed to make it more smooth and appealing.*

*Many times he could not make it as good as he wanted. Both his local colleagues and the local printing partners did not pay much attention to details, he said.*

Yes, their standards are different.

The "messy reality" is another factor calling for micromanagement. Things usually are not systematic here. There is a lot of manual work, and things need to be solved on a case-by-case basis.

*"Expats should understand that things are not systematic here yet. Many things need to set up, even in international companies, such as technology, rules and regulations,"* a repat finance manager of an international company says.

Subsequently, it is imperative for expats to micromanage.

This is simply something they must endure when working in Myanmar.

**Summary**

|  | Expats | Locals |
|---|---|---|
|  | Are strict about meeting times. Are strict about meeting deadlines. | Are not used to keeping schedules properly. Think that it is all too rigid and feel pressured. |
| Solutions | Remind local colleagues of the plan and monitor progress on a regular basis. Shorten deadlines. Train them to make to-do-lists, daily, weekly, monthly. | |
| Solutions (long-term) | Share about international standards and professionalism, the negative consequences of failing to do so for the whole process and organization. Provide Time Management Training. | |

## 7.2 HOW TO BE ON THE GROUND

As mentioned in Chapter 4 – What Locals Think about Foreigners – there are times when local colleagues think expats do not understand Myanmar at all. They put down the reason for this as: *"These expats never listen."*

One HR manager with over seven years' experience working with expats in Myanmar shares her story about such an expat:

*One of our expats is from an ASEAN country and is in charge of the marketing department.*

*At first, we liked him, as he seemed to be friendly. After a while, though, we started to feel like he thinks he is the master and we are the servants. Whenever a decision is needed, he never discusses or negotiates with us. He just orders us around!*

*For example, he wanted to send a marketing executive to a city in the north to do a small survey about customer behaviours there. The girl has good English skills and some relevant research experience.*

*However, sending her there alone is not appropriate as it would be dangerous for her. That is our culture. But he did not consult any of us and decided it this way.*

*The girl's family rejected that trip and demanded that the girl had to stop working there if she had to make those kinds of trips.*

*Eventually, the expat had to change his decision and send a guy for that trip.*

### ROLL UP MY SLEEVES AND GET MY HANDS DIRTY

One executive expat working in Thailand and Myanmar says, *"I am not hesitant to roll my sleeves and get my hands dirty."* This is a practical working method for expats in Myanmar.

Below is a story about how an expat misunderstood his local colleagues due to disconnecting with the reality on the ground:

*One local professional from a diplomatic organization shares that his previous supervisor (a Western expat) frequently thought that he was doing a lot of his subordinate's job.*

*It happened when he had to meet lots of local businessmen. In the job description it stated that this was his subordinate's job. He did not realize the local customs - those people want to meet directly with decision-makers. They did not think that there was a real delegation of authority from him to his subordinate. (As mentioned previously, delegation is not common in most Myanmar companies that are still family-style businesses.)*

*The direct meetings made things move quicker and helped him to achieve his goals more effectively.*

## AVOID THE COMMON CULTURAL CONFLICT IN MYANMAR

"No reporting of bad news and avoidance of confrontation" is a very common cultural conflict in Myanmar, as mentioned. Myanmar people have a different attitude towards conflict.

In such scenarios, being "on the ground" and monitoring progress is indispensable to foresee and prevent negative outcomes that will not be reported.

The story in Chapter 2, article 2.4 indicates that if the finance expat manager was in closer touch with the reality, he would have known that his local colleague had met with various kinds of obstacles working with multiple key stakeholders. There are many errors in operation in Myanmar.

*The finance expat manager was not happy, thinking that his financial analyst was chatting too much with friends over the phone in the office in Burmese.*

*He did not know that she was trying to chase local clients to register vendors' information into their new system. Further, she met difficulties dealing with other colleagues in the joint venture who were government officers. She could not tell them what to do and how to do it or impose deadlines on them. In the meantime, there were many demands from internal parties remote from Myanmar.*

*All this added up to her enduring a heavy workload. She, however, avoided a confrontation with her supervisor about how to solve the problem or to ask for his assistance. Instead, the lady tried to do everything herself.*

*She had an outburst when things went wrong, and she resigned.*

*Only then did the expat manager understand all the things she had been going through.*

The more "on the ground" expats are, the better for them in order to diagnose the reality and comprehend it. Assumptions do not work. The reality in Myanmar is very obscure unless one is audacious enough to "get his hand dirty."

At the beginning of an expat's tenure, it would be useful to observe and comprehend local colleagues - the way they work, the way they think, how they feel in different situations. It provides a real tie-in between expats and the "ground" of Myanmar. It is a good chance to plug into and learn from actuality; indirect reference sources cannot offer that much.

Subsequently, without a constant connection to the ground, one would easily drift away from reality and make mistakes.

Are you ready to roll up your sleeves and get your hands dirty?

**Summary**

|  | Expats | Locals |
|---|---|---|
|  | Do not follow progress. Cannot solve the issues when they start and are small. Things may grow worse. | No reporting of bad news, are afraid and try to keep things hidden. Do not want to confront to solve conflicts. |
| Solutions | Do not scold the person reporting bad news. Try to comprehend the real issues (ask questions) and help him to solve problems. | |
| Solutions (long-term) | Establish good relationships with local colleagues. Encourage local colleagues to report bad news and confront supervisors to find out solutions. Explain the positive aspects of reporting bad news on time and the negative aspects of avoidance of reporting bad news. Provide Critical Thinking and Problem-Solving training. | |

## 7.3 HOW TO RECRUIT IN A CULTURE YOU DO NOT COMPLETELY UNDERSTAND

Recruitment is tough in Myanmar, especially for international companies. The Talent Gold Rush (Chapter 3, article 3.4) happened when Foreign Direct Investment flowed strongly into Myanmar in recent times. There is a big gap between demand for and supply of local talent.

Under such circumstances, companies have to find out ways to navigate the talent shortage: recruiting potential candidates with the right attitude and training them so that they can do the job, for example. A crucial note is that it is better not to tell candidates bluntly that they lack appropriate skills. That is too discouraging.

Some companies, in order to retain local talent, require long maintenance contracts with conditions such as bonuses which will only be given after two or three years.

Besides salary, other factors such as the company's reputation and culture, bonuses, insurance, allowances (transportation, meals, etc), working hours, and office locations are taken into consideration by local candidates. If a company is too far from home, e.g., a two hours commute in the terrible Yangon traffic, a candidate will change jobs. Thus, companies in remote areas (i.e., North Dagon) will find it more challenging to find talent. Nowadays people prefer Saturday off, as far as working hours go, to achieve a work-life balance.

Many job sites make it easier to find candidates. Myjobs.com.mm, jobnet.com.mm (senior roles), jobsinyangon.com (small and medium-sized companies) are helpful. There are executive search agencies for management roles. For local candidates at the average level, VAC is a popular resource.

The current stagnant economy has somewhat lessened the pressure on companies to hire talent. The skill level of the local workforce has improved too, and the returns of repats are increasing. Plus, there have not been as many alluring new job opportunities as before.

## Summary

|  | Expats | Locals |
|---|---|---|
|  | Demand international standards of experience and skills. | Are in lack of them. Talent supply in shortage. |
| Solutions | Hire candidates with capacity less than requirements but who have the right attitude. Provide coaching on the job. | |
| Solutions (long-term) | Offer good working conditions (Saturdays off, transportation, insurance, etc. provided). Contract encourages a more extended period of working by awarding further incentives. Provide training. | |

## 7.4 HOW TO BE "LESS DEMANDING, MORE COACHING AND TRAINING"

Chapter 3, article 3.4 presents the long list of missing skills in Myanmar. They are IT basic (Excel, Word) to how to use computerized software, English, Communications, Problem Solving, Time Management, Critical Thinking, Creative Thinking, Leadership, Teamwork, Presentation, and more.

As such, locals reasonably expect that they can learn a lot from expats who have much more advanced knowledge and experience in their field.

At the same time, expats may be thought of as "too demanding" in that they expect things beyond the capacity of locals.

It is great to be less demanding and to give more coaching and training.

An assistant manager of a telecom company shares her story with an expat finance manager:

*My direct supervisor is from a neighboring country in Asia, and he is much too demanding.*

*He requires us to make a lot of inventory financial reports in our asset management function, with details that we do not have enough data and time to provide. He wants all to be upgraded in the system when we lack lots of skills for it. He does not ask me about my difficulties.*

*We come home very late every day. I feel stressed and tired.*

*He should listen to us that in Myanmar the company has been operating for only four years, while in his country it has been running for 20 years.*

*How can he expect us to be that professional?*

*If he gives me detailed guidance, I will do it better and faster.*

An HR repat with four years' experience working in Japan shares the story of how he tried to coach his local colleagues about time management:

*He applied the exact timing of Japanese people which he had learned from the time he worked there.*

*He advised them to have a schedule, a to-do list every day listing what to do, when, with whom, where, how, etc.*

*When people have their schedule and specific goals on a daily basis, they know how to value their time; they know how to value other people's time.*

*In case of meeting with another person – if someone comes late, he or she should inform the other person in advance.*

*"Thinking should be changed in Myanmar about being on time to conform to international standards," he asserted.*

Another critical skill - to "think outside the box" is also desirable. Notably, a kind of mental block prevents Myanmar people from taking initiatives and assuming higher responsibilities. Helping them to overcome the mental block is critical. It can only be done with the trust that comes from building relationships. When people feel trusted, comfortable, and are warmly received for whatever ideas they come up with, without the need to worry about "challenging seniors or elders," they are more confident to speak out about their opinions or new ideas. They become more proactive and responsible.

Currently, there is a favorite book among locals in Yangon on how to change the worried mindset. It is *The Art of Not Giving a F\*ck*. A Burmese version is available with a more polite title: *The Art of Not Giving a Care*. Expats would do well to advise local colleagues to read this to help overcome their mental block.

Besides coaching on the job, training courses are needed for the local workforce, either from internal sources or training organizations.

133

## Summary

|  | Expats | Locals |
|---|---|---|
|  | Demand international standards of experience and skills. | Are in lack of them. Talent supply in shortage. |
| Solutions | Less demanding. More coaching. | |
| Solutions (long-term) | Provide training. Hire a good HR manager for dealing with recruitment, learning and development, retaining talent and labor-related government relations. | |

# CHAPTER 8

# HOW TO FIX THE DAMAGE DONE AND JOURNEY TOWARD HEALTHY RELATIONSHIPS

## 8.1 HITTING THE WALL

Many expats think that Myanmar is a very challenging market in which to work. They feel this when they compare Myanmar with other countries they have worked in before, including other ASEAN countries.

**"Frustrating"** is a common word used to describe the situation.

### *OPPORTUNITIES VERSUS CHALLENGES IN THE LAND OF DISGRUNTLEMENT*

Expats can contribute their expertise and experience in Myanmar in many different ways. Things have just started in this new phase of the Golden Land's history.

Expats are coming here more and more. The door is open!

Many business people have found since the opening in 2012 that this last frontier market is full of opportunities. In every sector, new businesses can be set up and grow, even while recognizing the limited level of local development in that sector.

Yet after a while, digging more deeply into the market or investing here, they come upon more and more obstacles.

As mentioned, infrastructure shortcomings include such as things as intermittent electricity, lack of potable water, inadequate roads, and heavy traffic. Further, the lack of a skilled local workforce is a challenge. There is also a changing legal environment. Costs of living are high. Many locals who are would-be business partners or consumers have a traditional mindset. The weather is harsh - the hottest temperature may be 45 degrees Celcius in April, the time of the Thingyan festival.

In addition to those considerations, there are the language and cultural barriers.

Working here is truly not easy without understanding and accepting local culture and the country's overall situation.

### *"I WANT TO KILL PEOPLE EVERY DAY"*

Expats encounter various hindrances on a daily basis. Some even say: "*I hit a wall every day.*" The higher their expectations are, the more disappointed they feel. Everything seems to be so slow here, and it is hard to make things move.

There are sad stories about expats who resigned and left Myanmar shortly after arriving here, some after only one month, three months or six months.

A European expat says that when he first came here four years ago, he had the daily feeling: "*I want to kill people.*" He works for a local major business group which is aspiring to upgrade itself to the next level of development and meet international standards of doing business.

*I want to move things (that is why I am here), but to persuade people to follow new systems and practices is really tough, if not impossible. Resistance to change is not uncommon, as pre-existing rules and regulations are never questioned.*

*Many people in management, who are the ones who need to change first, are very close to the business owner, i.e., they are friends or family. Thus, they know their power. They do not want to lose their power, and they try to protect it by sticking to the previous way of doing business.*

*It is destructive and goes against all efforts to make things progress.*

*I work with other expats, and I have seen how some suffer because of the cultural barriers. The more they push for things to change, the more the system pushes back, and they cannot get anything done. After a short time, they leave. Sometimes it is just small things, like the fact that local employees simply do not reply to your emails. It's incredibly frustrating.*

## 8.2 ...AND BOUNCING BACK

There are, however, smiles after grievance and endurance.

The same European expat who has worked for a local business group for over six years was recently promoted to the top senior role of the group. He is the CEO.

How could he survive and be promoted in the land of disgruntlement?

### ACCEPTANCE, RESPECT, MUTUAL UNDERSTANDING, AND TRUST

He shares that for the first two months when he came here, he focused on seeking to understand the reality on the ground through interviewing people.

What other keys to success does he have?

*I have been respectful but do tell the truth to the owner who hires me.*

*Accept reality, even if you do not understand at first. Be humble. Listen. Observe critically.*

*I don't assume things.*

*Every time I thought I had gotten one step ahead, I found out that a step back was needed, as well. I then had to accept that change takes time and that I had to appreciate what had been achieved.*

*To transform a huge organization, changes should be simple and easy to implement.*

*I was making many mistakes, including installing a new HR system for over a thousand employees. The project was too complicated for the system to absorb. I was pushing too much, and it did not work.*

*Further, for a sizable organization, change is best done partially, in some advanced/progressive department or function first.*

*There is no need for it all to be done at the same pace.*

There are various strategies and methods an expat could employ when working in Myanmar, depending on their particular working environment and the business requirement.

The short stories below will briefly capture how two expats navigated the reality in Myanmar triumphantly.

### BUILDING AN EFFECTIVE LOCAL WORKFORCE

An ASEAN expat who has lived here for over three years is happy at the end of her contract. She successfully led the operation of her logistic service, achieving the business goals and re-structuring the Myanmar branch into a new organization of over 25 employees.

The local colleagues have been making a lot of improvements and now are much more skillful in various professional areas. They are confident in dealing with clients and have a spirit of teamwork. Only two employees resigned during a time when employees at most companies were changing positions every six months to a year. It is indeed a very positive number!

*This is a reputable worldwide company. When I started here, there were less than ten people.*

*The staff was usually not confident in dealing with clients and liked relying on the manager (myself) to make decisions whenever there was an issue. (Then I had to do "micromanagement".)*

*When a new customs system was applied in 2015, the pressure came not only from clients but also from the regional office, which generally would be described as "does not know Myanmar yet." I felt like they expected Myanmar to be at the same speed as other markets, while it is an entirely new one.*

*For me, working from day to night, through the whole week except for Sunday afternoon, was normal.*

*Of course, many times I felt stressful, frustrated, and had to be very patient.*

*One of the lucky things is that I have outstanding support from the mother company, where I have worked for over 12 years, since graduating from university. I proposed lots of training for employees to be provided by the company, such as teamwork, customer service, five whys for critical thinking, and time management, together with other technical training. I conducted lots of on-the-job training to local colleagues.*

*Further, I delegate tasks to them so that they are more responsible and confident in their roles.*

*The company also provides a benefit remuneration system to employees.*

### BUILDING MUTUAL TRUST AND EASING THINGS

The next example is from a Western general manager with a tourism service company.

*He has lived here over 12 years. His travel and tour company has grown and been able to keep employees for a long time – now there are 40 staff members, and only a few have resigned after five years. They are not paid higher than their competitors, though. They stay because they like working there.*

*They have a group of local business partners – service providers – that are co-operating with them very closely and cordially.*

*"Among lots of training that we provide to employees, there is special communication training such as 5W and 1H, how to compose messages, make videos, files, etc. They communicate a lot with international clients on a daily basis.*

*With local partners, we establish mutual trust via various prior co-operations. Surprisingly, we now work with 12 service providers without a contract.*

*It seems weird but thanks to that, whenever we want to provide a new tour to clients, we can deploy it very quickly. It is because the service providers and we do not have to go through the negotiation and contract signing process, which would be very time-consuming. We trust each other.*

*It is even quicker to deploy a new service in Myanmar than in other existing markets of our international companies in Europe or South East Asia."*

He summarizes his principles for success in Myanmar as the five ones below:

1. *Make staff feel at EASE.*
2. *Keep things SIMPLE (easy to apply).*
3. *Be EASY GOING (not too strict, not punitive for making mistakes).*
4. *Contribute to SUSTAINABLE development (things good for the country and people).*
5. *TRUST people without being naïve.*

## 8.3 HOW TO FIX THE DAMAGE DONE

### *To err is human*

It is impossible not to make mistakes when you work in a new country. (You will make mistakes even in your home country). But what do you do when you have made a mistake in your working relationship with local colleagues? How can you repair the damage?

There are two kinds of mistakes: short-term ones and long-term ones.

## SHORT TERM MISTAKES

A short-term mistake would be shouting at a local colleague or putting your feet on the table.

If you, with no ill intention, put your leg on the table and then realize you have offended local colleagues, it would be good to apologize to the people around you and state that you by no means meant any offense, you simply forgot the cultural taboo. You can mention that the action is quite usual in your country and many others, but that you want to respect the fact that it is not acceptable here.

If you shouted at a local colleague and thus caused him to lose face, an apology, at least, is needed. Apologizing directly to that person, however, would make the issue even more complicated.

One HR manager who has many years working in international and joint ventures organization advises that you made an **"indirect" apology** to that person.

Myanmar culture focuses on indirectness, rather than straightforwardness. (Chapter 1, Article 1.3 – gentle indirectness.)

So one of the things you could do is ask him to go to lunch or dinner with you, or show in some other way that you care about him.

Please remember to do this in front of other people, to help him "Save Face".

In the background, people will think that, yes, you were shouting at him, but then you appreciated him again. The appreciative gesture would offset the negative one.

One should not make use of this device often, of course.

*There is a story of an expat who shouted at his subordinate and apologized to him later. That was all right. Yet the expat could not control his temper when there was too much pressure. It started to repeat itself like a cycle. The expat would shout and then apologize. After more than three times of this cycle, the local colleague resigned. He was unable to stand the frequent shouting of his manager.*

Also, it is important to know that the higher the rank of the victim who has been shouted at, the more difficult it is to forgive as he or she has "Lost Face" in a heavier way because of his or her preceding good reputation and high profile. (Please refer to Chapter 1, Article 1.3.)

### LONG-TERM MISTAKES

One beautiful day, after reading this book, you realize that building good relationships with your local colleagues is essential to your success in Myanmar. Yet you have been making the long-term mistake of being distant toward them.

What to do?

**Just do it.** Apply the advice in this book or from other reliable sources.

Over time your local colleagues will realize your goodwill and respond. Myanmar people, for the most part, do not harbor deep hatred. Their generosity, rooted in Buddhism, allows them to forgive people. This is in line with their belief that good and generous deeds will benefit them in the next life. They have more sympathy for foreigners as guests and understand that they may not know Myanmar culture well.

There is a Myanmar proverb – *Please forgive someone for making a mistake just one time.*

It will take time, however, and your recent actions of goodwill will require effort and time to make amends for the previous cold period.

As mentioned in Chapter 6 – Show Your Care and Kindness – it is good to be interested in them, to care for them, ask questions about their career dreams, their family, their parents, spouses, children, etc. Mingle with them, go to meals together without a business purpose. Take part in their events such as birthdays, donations, family funerals, festivals, etc.

All this is to build friendly relationships and to show that you are kind and that you genuinely care about them and their lives as people and friends, not just as co-workers.

It needs to be done with sincerity, though.

Stephen Covey, the author of *The Seven Habits of Highly*

*Successful People,* puts it: *"We are trusted because of our way of doing things, not because of our polished exteriors or our expertly crafted communications."*

## 8.4 JOURNEY TOWARDS A HEALTHY RELATIONSHIP WITH LOCAL COLLEAGUES

*THE FEMININE CULTURE AND THE SUCCESSFUL WORKPLACE*

As spoken about in Chapter 6, a feminine culture values feminine characteristics, such as co-operation and caring, more than achieving goals. It emphasizes happiness over competition.

Thus, a successful workplace in Myanmar is based on building personal relationships, establishing mutual trust, and celebrating group achievements.

*NO EXPECTATIONS, AND BE PATIENT*

It is not uncommon that expats here have to reduce their expectations about the performances of local colleagues. It is best to have no expectations and to accept things as they are.

It means that one needs to be very patient.

Below is the story of a group marketing manager for an international brand. He is an ASEAN expat who has been working in Myanmar successfully during his two-year contract period.

*"When I first came here, I was surprised to see two cases where local colleagues resigned after being shouted at or scolded by expats. I asked around to understand the phenomenon. Eventually, I concluded that 'It is hard to maintain talent, but easy to lose it', given that there are lots of new opportunities for the young people here these days.*

*I decided to be very calm and patient all the time. I try never to show anger or scold people. Instead, I open the door for queries from my local colleagues, that they can ask me as much as they can. One time, two times, five or more times, all are fine. They can ask until they are clear about their assignments.*

*Further, I do 'Triple Check' of Yes. The 1st one is to make sure they hear me, the 2nd one is to make sure they understand it, and the 3rd one is to see that they do it.*

*I do micromanagement, of course. I break down projects into tasks and follow up on local colleagues. I cannot just give them the strategy, plan, and goals and then wait.*

*Also, I try to encourage them, even on small good things they do. For example, I praise one who has an idea of giving a rose to a customer buying our beauty care products at a holiday festival.*

*It has taken great effort for me - I have to be ten times more patient than in my home country."*

## DON'T BE IN THE "EXPAT GHETTO"

There are stories about expats who have lived in Myanmar for a long time, i.e., five years, seven years or more, but who are still very "expat."

A Westerner told me that he has a friend who organizes inbound tours for Europeans in Myanmar. This friend has lived here for five years but never has been to a local restaurant or a street food shop.

Another one shares about an American expat working in the economic development sector who was surprised to know that locals eat with their hands. The expat had been working here for years.

Those people seem very "expat"; they are alien to the Myanmar culture and people.

How can a person live in a country for years at a time and not know the basic "nuts and bolts" of the place where they live? Probably they only live in the **"expat ghetto"**.

Local professionals suggest expats mingle with locals more. Many expats do not spend time with local colleagues outside of the job. Sometimes it is good just to get together in groups. It would be great to organize monthly gatherings with locals and not talk about business; just use the time to get to know more about each other personally.

Unearthing or decoding the reality of a situation brings its reward.

Here is a funny story of a friend of mine who came from Europe:

*He was curious about a kind of fruit with yellow colors, with a hard cover that looked like a hedgehog's hide, and which had a unique smell.*

*He was too shy to try it when it was sold on the street, even though he is very cosmopolitan and has traveled and taught in more than a hundred countries in the world, including years in Africa.*

*Eventually, after trying it once, he enjoyed it very much! Now he even buys it to bring to friends.*

*It is durian! They like it, too!*

You may miss out on lots of good things without an "audacious" mindset. It requires a bit of a daring attitude for many expats to blend into the local scene in Myanmar.

Further, learning the local language is one way to bridge the gap. At least knowing enough language to survive is helpful when necessary, and your local colleagues will be happy to see you make the effort to study Burmese.

*"If you talk to a man in a language he understands, that goes to his head. If you talk to him in his language, that goes to his heart."* (Nelson Mandela)

Beyond any doubt, though, be prepared for being laughed at when you first utter some Burmese!

## *MEETING THE LOCAL NEED FOR NEW SKILLS AND KNOWLEDGE*

Crucially, many HR Heads and other local professionals suggest that expats train their local colleagues more. Local professionals believe that because expats are from much more advanced countries, they have lots of international qualifications and experience and can help them achieve professional skills and gain knowledge of international standards. Such training indeed will help them improve their performance, and it, in turn, supports the expats' missions.

Myanmar people are very eager to acquire precious knowledge. They have such local proverbs as: "*Knowledge is valuable like a pot of gold*", "*Never too old to gain new knowledge*", and "*There is no light as bright as knowledge*".

One senior finance repat shares her view on many expats working in her international company:

"*I think they have the pressure of a contract term regarding time, i.e., two years or three years; thus they do not have enough time to teach or train local colleagues thoroughly or sincerely. It is understandable, for they need to survive the current position first. However, it makes the relationship worse than it would be otherwise.*"

Indeed, the capacity to train locals in new skills, techniques, and knowledge is the expats' advantage in relations with local colleagues.

### TAKING TIME FOR BUILDING TRUST

*"Trust is the glue of life. It is the most essential ingredient in effective communication. It is the foundation principle that holds all relationships."* (Stephen Covey, *The Speed of Trust*)

Like any relationship, the relationships between locals and expats require respect, mutual understanding, acceptance, and ultimately trust. Trust is the ultimate goal in fostering a relationship. Without trust, it is impossible.

An HR head of an international company shares that her previous American general manager was an outstanding leader:

*"He was honest, respectful, and patient. He trusted people. He showed his leadership – he led people through difficulties to achieve goals and accepted his responsibilities. If there was a mistake, he did not blame others.*

*He kept his word once he promised to do something. For example, he promised to raise the insurance coverage for employees to twenty times higher; he delivered it. It was tough for him to negotiate with the regional office to keep that promise, though.*

*We knew we could trust him.*

*We all co-operated with him well. We wanted to support him to make the business a significant success!"*

For her, the current expat general manager (GM) is in contrast to the previous one:

*"Our current GM is a Westerner. He, however, does not seem to trust people. Whenever we (managers) submit proposals for him to decide on, he asks too many detailed questions. He asks, "Why?", "Why?", and "Why?"*

*He does not keep his word. For example, he required us to work during Thingyan, but when the holidays came, he did not show up while we were waiting for him, without any explanation.*

*This didn't happen just once. How can we trust him?"*

Keeping one's promises is one of the critical factors in building trust with local colleagues. If you do not "walk the talk" it is hard for them to believe your words in the future. Trust is possible only when actions reflect words. Communication is possible when trust exists.

How long does it take to build up healthy and trusting relationships between locals and expats - ones in which locals feel comfortable to report bad news and confront their expat supervisors to find solutions for problems?

One HR Head (a Myanmar national) of a telecom-related European company, who has over six years of experience working with expats, estimates:

*"It would take about six months in fast progress. Otherwise, it would be about one year."*

The process would need to include separate monthly meetings with individuals at work, then at lunch or dinner, and other positive sessions where they only encourage and ask how they can help local colleagues.

Showing you care in an honest manner is essential. When people know you care genuinely about their interests as much as your own, they will trust you. If they think you are out for yourself only, they may think 'Be watchful of that person.'

Empathy is critical - it is important to make local colleagues feel comfortable and not afraid of harsh judgment.

A lot of tolerance, encouragement, and patience is required.

### Summary – A framework for building relationships with local colleagues

|  | Expats | Locals |
|---|---|---|
|  | Dos and Don'ts for local colleagues. | Know in advance their supervisors' expectation. |
|  | Eschew a judgemental manner. | Feel glad, comfortable, and respected. |
| Solutions | Separate meetings with individuals, positive meetings (only to encourage).<br>Monthly gatherings outside of work.<br>Coach on the job.<br>Keep your word. | |
| Solutions (long-term) | Provide Training.<br>Mingle with locals.<br>Participate in cultural events, festivals, and join donation and charity activities.<br>Study Burmese. | |

## 8.5 SUGGESTIONS FOR WINNING

*"The international manager reconciles cultural dilemmas."* (Fons Trompenaars, a leading scholar on intercultural theories).

Many expats in Myanmar have a plan to work and live here a long time. In fact, the longer they stay here, the more advantage they have as "having Myanmar experience". The length of stay indicates how much they have accepted, adapted, and developed here.

The ability to overcome cultural challenges in overseas assignments is a "must-have" characteristic for a successful expatriate. In Myanmar, this can only happen through establishing very positive relationships with locals.

The strategy for expats to overcome cultural challenges varies, depending on their purpose for working in Myanmar and the length of their tenure, and if they want to live here for long.

For example, with a two-year contract and without knowing if one wants to extend their contract here, learning Basic Burmese is possible in 20 hours. But with a five-year contract, learning intermediate level Burmese would be a good goal.

The below recommendations cover the basic level to further levels of winning the confidence and trust of local colleagues (Not necessarily in this order):

## 1. *SHARE WITH LOCAL COLLEAGUES THAT YOU ARE AWARE OF MYANMAR CULTURE AND RESPECT IT.*

Encourage discussion of problems and solutions between locals and foreigners. Create a feedback mechanism and follow it.

Provide your expectations of how your local colleagues should behave in accordance with basic international standards. Address their attitude towards conflict – especially when it comes to reporting bad news and confrontation.

Share and exchange information, as well as goals, objectives, and the procedures of your function.

## 2. *BUILD RELATIONSHIPS*

Maintain monthly working meetings with direct reports, and organize gatherings outside of work (without talking about business).

Understand their religion, ethnicity, family situation, parents, spouse, lover, children, home locations, hobbies, and characteristics.

## 3. *FOLLOW THE GUIDE "HOW TO SUCCEED IN THE WORKPLACE" - COMMUNICATIONS (VERBAL AND NON-VERBAL) AND MANAGEMENT (CHAPTERS 5,6,7).*

Provide coaching on international standards to local colleagues.

## 4. INTEGRATE INTO THE LOCAL CULTURE; AVOID THE "EXPAT GHETTO" TRAP.

- Read culture and history books.
- Eat at local restaurants and street food shops sometimes (vegetarian food is safer).
- Wear local clothes sometimes, using local services such as handymen, seamstresses.
- Keep track of economic and political events, go to pagodas and temples regularly with local friends; visit their home and invite them to your home.
- Learn the language (survival level of 20 hours) to intermediate level. Have a local name.
- Find local friends (maybe repats) and go to local events (i.e., pagodas, concerts, art exhibits).
- Travel around Myanmar.
- Make donations and participate in volunteer activities (i.e., in professional groups or helping the related government department).
- Exchange culture (souvenirs, knowledge, food, etc.).

## NOTE:

1. In an organization, if expats have enough authority to do so, they should combine these things into the company manual as guidance for professional behaviours.

2. Adaptation does not mean capitulation. While adapting to the local culture, expats can communicate their

expectations regarding their roles' goals and processes. Further, the expat can be critical and demanding when appropriate (after having carefully assessed the situation and the influencing factors). Each can have his own method of confronting situations of inappropriate behaviors.

## A SMALL NOTE ON MINGLING WITH LOCALS

*"No one is useless in this world who lightens the burdens of another."* (Charles Dickens)

An expat may very well be lonely here if he or she only relies on relationships with other expats in Myanmar.

Any expat acquaintances are also subject to a contract term, meaning they will leave Myanmar after a short period. It is hard to find true friendships without spending time cultivating them. Further, other expats also come from alien countries. International bars and restaurants are familiar places where they mingle.

Many expats I met here confessed to a kind of "floating" sentiment of living here without family and close friends. They feel like "Nowhere is home!" Though they are wealthy, they feel life is meaninglessness from time to time.

The experience may be different if they have local friends. This is particularly true in cases where one takes time to join local cultural events, either holidays or charity activities, to experience the very "real" life of locals. These are the authentic lives of people who have suffered from a dark history of repression and the current constraints of being citizens of a country ranked as one of the poorest countries in the world. At the same time, Myanmar is the most generous country in the world, too.

Helping the people here, who are still in a daily battle to meet their basic needs, is a good cause that will give meaning and purpose to life in Myanmar.

# A NOTE FOR THE BOOK

As the book embarks on its mission to support expats in overcoming the cultural challenges to succeed in Myanmar, making generalizations about the local culture is a must to enable the comprehension of it. They are, nonetheless, only crystallized conclusions about the diversified dimensions and nuances of a culture, not rigid rules.

Culture is very "mosaic". Everyone that you meet is a unique person whose behaviors reflect the rules and principles in the book at times and not at other times.

Your "on-the-ground" feelings and thoughts about people are crucial then. Believe in your own judgment!

*Finally, thank you for joining me on the journey through the book. If you find it useful, I would really appreciate if you spare a minute to spread the word. Readers like you make a huge difference to helping new readers find helpful resources for them.*

*Below is the link to the e-book:*

*https://www.amazon.com/When-Global-Meets-Local-Expatriates-ebook/dp/B07MXV92W7*

*Thank you!*
*Hana Bui*

# ABOUT THE AUTHOR AND INTERCULTURAL WORKSHOPS

Hana Bui is an intercultural trainer and author. She was an entrepreneur for many years. Currently living in Yangon, Hana likes wearing eingyi, eating Burmese food and can converse in Burmese. Myanmar has become her home.

As an expat working in the Golden Land in HR services for six years, Hana realizes that there are always cultural struggles between expats and the local amiable people (herself included), particularly when the expats first arrive. They can only achieve success by overcoming their biggest challenges here - the cultural conflicts.

Her book then was born to assist expats to work in harmony with the Burmese in order to succeed.

*When Global Meets Local - How Expatriates Can Succeed in Myanmar: A First-Time Guidebook.*

The book is indeed a combination of her strong desire to help people to solve their problems and her writing passion. She has been fond of writing since a teenager. Her mother was a librarian and she read voraciously for free since she was a little child. She also spent some years as an independent business journalist in Ho Chi Minh City, Vietnam, where she comes from.

Hana sees herself as a cultural bridge between Myanmar and the world. She has actually developed a strong interest in global-local interrelations since ten years ago when she did an MA degree on Globalization and Communications at University of Leicester, England.

Hana's simple and applicable approach is employed in the book for busy expats readers. The same approach is used for her 1-day "Cultural Integration" workshops for expatriates in Myanmar.

For inquiries about the book or the above workshops, please contact *hanabui.mm@gmail.com.*

Link to "About the author":
http://amazon.com/author/hanabui

# THE APPENDIX

There are several key facts about Myanmar that expats should not miss knowing. Also, the author suggests some new and easy ways to discover the culture and people in Yangon.

## 1. DOS AND DON'TS IN MYANMAR
https://www.tripsavvy.com/dos-and-donts-in-myanmar-1629596

## 2. LOCAL RESTAURANTS & STREET FOOD
Lucky 7, corner of Anawrahta and 49th street, Yangon.
Shwe Pu Zun, No 246-248 Anawrahta, Lanmadaw Township, Yangon.
Street food Breakfast (6 a.m. – 10 a.m., Indian Vegetarian), corner of Anawrahta and 46th street, Botataung Township, Yangon.

## 3. LEARNING BURMESE (SHOULD STUDY WITH A LOCAL TEACHER).
John O'kell is the leading scholar in the Burmese study field.
https://www.quora.com/What-are-the-best-resources-for-learning-Burmese
https://www.soas.ac.uk/sea/burmese/studymaterials/suppliers/

## 4. EVENTS TO TAKE PART IN

Holidays and festivals

https://www.tripsavvy.com/myanmar-essential-holidays-and-festivals-4125946

Charity activities:

Beik Hmam Shin Charity Association Bago

Phone 052 222 1326, Address 2418/2419 Teiktha Road, Mazin Quarter, Bago.

Facebook: Beik Mam Shin,

https://www.mmtimes.com/news/despair-delight.html

## 5. TRAVELLING IN YANGON – A NEW AND EASY ESCAPE TRIP

Yangon Circle Train

https://www.travelfish.org/sight_profile/burma_myanmar/yangon_and_surrounds/yangon_region/yangon/2060

http://yangon-rangoon.com/yangon-circular-train.html

Yangon Water Bus

https://www.facebook.com/yangonwaterbus/

https://www.tripadvisor.com/Attraction_Review-g294191-d13485190-Reviews-Yangon_Water_Bus-Yangon_Rangoon_Yangon_Region.html

Yangon Bus

https://www.myanmore.com/2017/08/ultimate-yangon-bus-ride/

# SELECTED BIBLIOGRAPHY

*ONLINE RESOURCES*

Myanmar (Burma) Personality Profile. (n.d). Retrieved from https://www.16personalities.com/country-profiles/myanmar-burma

Hays, J. (2014, May). Burmese Character. Retrieve from http://factsanddetails.com/southeast-asia/Myanmar/sub5_5c/entry-3039.html

Hanson, D. (2015). Thai Followship Kreng Jai Style. HQ Asia, Issue 9. Retrieved from https://hcli.org/articles/thai-followship-kreng-jai-style

Hays J. (n.d). Ne Win Years in Burma in the 1960s, 70s and 80s. Retrieved from http://factsanddetails.com/southeast-asia/Myanmar/sub5_5a/entry-3010.html

Livermore, D. (2010, January 6). CQ the Test of Your Potential for Cross-Cultural Success. Retrieved from https://www.forbes.com/2010/01/06/cq-cultural-intelligence-leadership-managing-globalization.html#75ead39725bb

In Search of High CQ – a trendy management idea for the age of Globalisation. (2010, April 6). Retrieved from https://www.economist.com/business/2010/04/06/in-search-of-high-cq

DuPraw M. & Axner M. (1997). Working on Common Cross-cultural Communication Challenges. Retrieved from http://www.pbs.org/ampu/crosscult.html#DISCLOSE

Brindle D. (2017, September 5). UK slips out of top 10 most generous nations as giving surges in developing countries. Retrieved from https://www.theguardian.com/voluntary-sector-network/2017/sep/05/uk-out-top-10-most-generous-nations-global-giving-index

Sivers D. & Nicholas Krapels N. (2014). New Information and Cultural Insights Entrepreneurs Need to Start a Business in Myanmar. [Kindle version]. Retrieved from Amazon.com

Vulpe T., Kealey D., Protheroe D., and MacDonald D. (2001). A Profile of the Interculturally Effective Person. (2nd ed). Canada: Department of Foreign Affairs and International Trade. Retrieved from http://www.international.gc.ca/cil-cai/publications.aspx?lang=eng

Taylor K. (n.d). The Day Of The Week You Were Born Says Everything About Your Personality. Retrieved from https://www.littlethings.com/burmese-zodiac/

Cablido-Crugerl. (2018). Do's & Don'ts in Myanmar. Retrieved from https://www.tripsavvy.com/dos-and-donts-in-myanmar-1629596

Religious Beliefs In Myanmar (Burma). (n.d). Retrieved from https://www.worldatlas.com/articles/religious-beliefs-in-myanmar-burma.html

Rudkin A. and Erba J. (2018, January). Myanmar Cultural Dimensions: Exploring the Relationship Among the Social Identity, Attitude Towards Globalization and Preferences of Myanmar Consumers in Yangon. International Journal of Asia Pacific Studies 14(1):191-226. Retrieved from http://ijaps.usm.my/?page_id=4018

Rarick C. and Nickerson I. (2006). An Exploratory Study of Myanmar Culture Using Hofstede's Value Dimensions. Retrieved from https://papers.ssrn.com/sol3/papers.cfm?abstract_id=1114625

Copland J. (n.d). On trade, tea and TVs: The Key To Myanmar's Consumer Market. Retrieved from http://www.tnsglobal.com/sites/default/files/TL_On%20trade%2C%20tea%20and%20TVs.pdf

Hofstede G. & Hostede G.J. & Minkov M. (2010). Cultures and Organizations: Software of the Mind (3rd ed). [Kindle version]. Retrieved from Amazon.com

## PRINT BOOKS AND NEWSPAPERS

Steinberg D. (2013). *Burma/Myanmar: What everyone needs to know*. (2nd ed.). New York: Oxford University Press.

Guruge A. and Dhammananda K. (2000). *Buddhism in Modern Life*.

Holmes H. and Tangtongtavy S. (2003). *Working with Thais*. (2nd ed). Bangkok: White Lotus.

Kyi Kyi May and Nugent N. (n.d). *Culture Smart Myanmar* (Burma). London: Kuperard.

Khin Myo Chit. (2016). *Colorful Myanmar* (5th ed). Yangon: Parami Bookshop.

Khin Myo Chit. (2015 November). *Cultural Heritage and Other Articles*. Yangon: Parami Bookshop.

Khin Maung Nuynt. (2005). *Myanmar Traditional Monthly Festivals*. Yangon: Innwa Publishing House.

Meiji, Soe. (2017). *Culture and Beyond Myanmar*. (3rd ed). Yangon: Sarpay Beikman.

Saw Myat Yin. (2011). *Culture Shock Myanmar: A Survival Guide to Customs and Etiquette*. Tarrytown, NW: Marshall Cavendish Editions.

Myanmar News Agency. (2018, June 20). President, First Lady, State Counsellor enshrine religious objects into Eternal Peace Pagoda. *The Global New Light of Myanmar*.

Myanmar News Agency. (2018, January 2). 18,000 monks consecrate Shwedagon. *The Global New Light of Myanmar.*